Contents

List of Contributors

Rosalyn Ashby   (Institute of Education, University of London)

Paul Black   (King's College, London)

Ezra Blondel   (King's College, London)

Margaret Brown   (King's College, London)

Alaric Dickinson   (Institute of Education, University of London)

Rosalind Driver   (University of Leeds)

Sandra Duggan   (University of Durham)

Richard Gott   (University of Durham)

Martin Hughes   (University of Exeter)

John Leach   (University of Leeds)

Peter Lee   (Institute of Education, University of London)

Fred Lubben   (University of York)

Robin Millar   (University of York)

Penny Munn   (University of Central Lancashire)

Phil Scott   (University of Leeds)

Shirley Simon   (King's College, London)

BERA DIALOGUES
Series Editor:

MULTILINGUAL MATTERS LTD
Clevedon • Philadelphia • Adelaide

Library of Congress Cataloging in Publication Data

Progression in Learning/Edited by Martin Hughes
BERA Dialogues: 11
1. Learning ability. 2. Child development. 3. Cognition in children.
4. Articulation (Education). I. Hughes, Martin. II. Series.
LB1134.P76   1995
370.15'23–dc20   95-23851

British Library Cataloguing in Publication Data

A CIP catalogue record for this book is available from the British Library.

ISBN 1-85359-310-9 (hbk)
ISBN 1-85359-309-5 (pbk)

Multilingual Matters Ltd

UK: Frankfurt Lodge, Clevedon Hall, Victoria Road, Clevedon, Avon BS21 7SJ.
USA: 1900 Frost Road, Suite 101, Bristol, PA 19007, USA.
Australia: P.O. Box 6025, 83 Gilles Street, Adelaide, SA 5000, Australia.

Typeset by Bookcraft, Stroud, Gloucestershire.
Printed and bound in Great Britain by the Cromwell Press.

Introduction

MARTIN HUGHES

This book is concerned with progression in learning. In other words, it is about the short-term and long-term changes in children's knowledge and understanding which take place as they progress through various domains of learning.

The book consists of five studies which look at progression in a range of different domains. In Chapter 1 Penny Munn is concerned with progression in preschool children's conceptions of literacy and numeracy. Shirley Simon, Margaret Brown, Paul Black and Ezra Blondel in Chapter 2 look at progression between the ages of 6 and 13 years in pupils' understanding of two distinct areas of mathematics and science. Chapter 3, by Peter Lee, Rosalyn Ashby and Alaric Dickinson, deals with progression between the ages of 7 and 14 years in pupils' ideas about historical enquiry and explanation. In Chapter 4 Robin Millar, Richard Gott, Fred Lubben and Sandra Duggan focus on progression between the ages of 9 and 14 years in pupils' abilities to carry out scientific investigations. Chapter 5, by John Leach, Rosalind Driver, Robin Millar and Phil Scott, looks at pupils' understanding of the nature of science between the ages of 9 and 16 years. Yet despite this diversity in the ages and topics being studied, there are, as we shall see, some important common themes arising from the chapters in this volume.

As with all contributions to the BERA Dialogues series, the aim of the book is to report findings from current educational research on issues of relevance to educational policy and practice. This introductory chapter therefore describes how and why the book came about, why the authors are interested in progression, how they have chosen to study progression, what their main findings are, and what the implications are for policy, practice and future research.

The ESRC Programme

This book has arisen directly from the work of a research programme funded by the Economic and Social Research Council (ESRC). The programme, entitled 'Innovation and Change in Education: The Quality of Teaching and Learning', was set up as a direct response to the changes in the UK education system which were brought about by the 1988 Education Reform Act. These changes included the introduction of a National Curriculum for all children aged 5–16 years; an associated programme of standardised national assessment; the devolvement of financial responsibility from local authorities to individual schools; and the encouragement of market forces through enhanced parental choice. The overall aim of the ESRC programme, it should be noted, was not to carry out an evaluation of these reforms, but rather to use them as a context in which to address some fundamental questions concerned with teaching and learning. Thus as well as an interest in progression, the programme has also been concerned with understanding the processes of change in educational establishments, and in understanding how teaching and learning are perceived by those most closely involved in it. Altogether, the ESRC funded ten projects at various centres in England and Scotland during the period 1991–5, as well as funding the author of this chapter to co-ordinate the programme. Further examples of the work of the programme can be found in two other edited books (Hughes, 1994, 1995), and in two special issues of the journal *Research Papers in Education* (volume 9, no. 2 and volume 10, no. 2).

The focus on progression in learning grew out of the common research interests of four of the ten projects in the programme (those based at the University of Strathclyde; at King's College, London; at the Institute of Education, London; and at the Universities of Durham and York). Concerns common to these projects were discussed at a series of programme workshops convened during 1992 and 1993. These workshops were expanded to include, among others, a project based at the Universities of Leeds and York which was focusing on progression in children's understanding of the nature of science: this project was also funded by the ESRC, but was not one of the ten projects originally funded as part of the Innovation and Change programme. As a result of these workshops, a symposium on 'Progression in Learning' was presented at the 1993 BERA Conference in Liverpool, and a similar symposium was presented at the 1994 Annual Meeting of the American Educational Research Association (AERA) in New Orleans. The chapters in this book have arisen directly from the papers presented at these two symposia.

Why Study Progression?

Underlying any curriculum is a model of progression. That is, any attempt to generate a sequence of teaching and learning activities in a particular domain must inevitably be based on some assumptions about what constitutes an appropriate order in which these activities should be presented to learners. In many cases, however, the model of progression is implicit rather than explicit. In other words, the assumptions being made about progression in learning are not articulated by the curriculum developers or teachers, but remain hidden from view.

The introduction of the National Curriculum in England and Wales, as a result of the 1988 Education Reform Act, made the notion of progression much more salient. Of particular significance was the recommendation of the Task Group on Assessment and Training (TGAT – DES, 1988) that all subjects within the National Curriculum should follow the same ten-level scale. The acceptance of this recommendation meant that the various subject groups charged with designing specific attainment targets and programmes of study had to pay explicit attention to levels of progression in their subject area. In other words, they had to generate an appropriate model of progression for their particular domain of learning.

In attempting to generate such a model of progression, a number of sources of information might be used. As several contributors to this book have pointed out, three of the main sources are the following:

1. The structure of knowledge in the learning domain itself. A conceptual analysis of particular topics within the domain might suggest – or even logically require – that a particular sequence should be followed. Thus, in mathematics an understanding of multiplication rests on a prior understanding of addition, so it would seem appropriate that addition should be taught first.

2. Practical classroom experience. Teachers or curriculum designers may have come to believe, as a result of their direct experience in the classroom, that pupils will learn more effectively if one activity comes before rather than after another activity, or that some learning experiences are more or less 'appropriate' for pupils at a particular age.

3. Empirical knowledge about children's learning. A body of knowledge may have accumulated concerning the ways in which learners normally make their way through a particular domain. This body of knowledge might be underpinned by general theories of intellectual development (such as that of Piaget) or by more specific theories

concerning particular types of learning (e.g. approaches to the teaching of reading): it might, however, be relatively atheoretical.

Our primary aim in this book is to contribute to the third of these three sources of information: that is, we want to add to what is known empirically about progression in learning. At the same time, we are aware that the three sources cannot be considered in isolation, and in practice are likely to be intertwined. For example, the authors of Chapters 2, 3 and 4 explicitly develop models of what might underlie progression in their respective domains – drawing both on previous research and on a careful analysis of the domain itself – before testing their models against actual data. The empirical findings generated in this way can, in turn, feed back into the development of further and more refined models: at the same time, we hope that they will be used to inform and enrich classroom practice.

The main issues being addressed in this book can now be specified. We want to know, across a range of learning domains, answers to questions such as the following:

1. What are the main changes in children's understanding as they progress through a particular domain?

2. How much variation is there between children in their levels of understanding? What might underlie such variation?

3. How does the understanding of individual children change over time? Does this follow an invariant sequence, or are different routes followed by different learners?

4. How far are these changes in understanding influenced by particular teaching or learning experiences?

Clearly, these questions represent a major agenda for research. We certainly do not claim to have provided definitive answers to any question in any domain; moreover, our attention has focused more on questions (1) and (2) than on questions (3) and (4). Nevertheless, we feel that the contributions in this book provide a useful basis both for clarifying the nature of the task and for providing some initial answers.

How Do We Study Progression?

Any attempt to answer questions such as those specified above inevitably raises a number of methodological issues. In this section we will consider three of the most pressing issues, and look at how they have been addressed by the various contributors to this book.

The first issue to consider is whether a study of progression needs to have a longitudinal design (in which the same children are studied over a period of time) or whether it is sufficient to have a cross-sectional design (in which different groups of children are studied at different ages). In answering this question, it is helpful to draw on a distinction made by Millar *et al.*, in Chapter 4. These authors point out that we can think about progression in terms of populations or in terms of individuals. If our interest is primarily with populations (as it might be if we were addressing questions (1) and (2) above) then it is appropriate to carry out cross-sectional studies which look at how different populations display different types of understanding at different ages. We can then use the data generated by such studies to construct models – at the population level – of how progression might take place between different levels of understanding. This approach is adopted by most of the contributors to this book. However, our concern might be primarily with the individual, and in understanding how progression takes place as an individual learner moves through a domain (for example, if our focus was on answering questions (3) and (4) above). In this case, then, we need to carry out longitudinal studies of individual children – the approach adopted by Munn in Chapter 1.

It is of course possible to combine the two methods, and this mixed approach is adopted by Simon *et al.*, in Chapter 2. Their study was based around a cross-sectional design, in that interview data were collected from different groups of children at Years 2, 4, 6 and 8. However, a short-term longitudinal design was superimposed on this cross-sectional design, in that the children were also observed during a 2/3 month period following the initial interviews. During this period they experienced a teaching input related to the topics being studied, and the children were then interviewed again at the end of this time. Clearly, a mixed design like this can throw light on progression both at the population level and at the individual level.

The question of whether we are primarily concerned with populations or with individuals is also relevant to the second methodological issue – whether children are studied in small groups, or whether they are studied on their own. Within this book, the use of small groups for data-gathering purposes is favoured by two of the research teams (see Chapters 4 and 5). The arguments for such an approach are that it more closely resembles classroom work, and that children might be more relaxed and forthcoming in the presence of their peers. The disadvantage of this approach is that it is much harder to identify the contribution of particular individuals to the overall outcome. Clearly, if our interest is in progression at the population level, then this disadvantage is less important. However, if our interest is with progression at the individual level, then it becomes a critical problem. If this is the case, then data must be collected from individuals – the approach adopted in Chapters 1 and 2 of this book. As before, a mixed approach is possible, and this is adopted by Lee, Ashby & Dickinson in the study described in Chapter 3. These authors interviewed children individually as well as making videotapes of them working in groups of three.

The third methodological issue to be considered here is in some ways the most intractable. It is the question of how we obtain a valid and reliable measure of children's understanding within a particular domain and at a particular age. The approach adopted by all the contributors to this book has been to design specific tasks intended to elicit children's understanding, and to present them to children – either individually or in small groups – outside of the classroom by members of the research team. In some cases the tasks are accompanied by in-depth questioning about why children have responded in a particular way. Children's performance on these tasks, or their response to the in-depth questioning, is then used as an index of their understanding.

For some time now, this approach has been subject to various criticisms from psychologists. These criticisms take two main forms. One line of criticism, which dates back to the 1970s (e.g. Donaldson, 1978), is that children's performance in such a situation may not be a reliable measure of their understanding. Children may be inhibited by the novelty of the situation; they may fail to understand the task requirements, or they may be overly concerned with giving answers which the researcher finds acceptable. This line of criticism, it should be noted, makes the assumption that there is such a thing as 'children's understanding', which can in principle be measured by some independent means. The second line of criticism, however, does not make this assumption. Rather, it assumes that all understanding is essentially 'situated' within certain contexts or social practices (e.g. Lave, 1988). From this point of view, it is a serious conceptual mistake to assume there is any relationship between the understanding which children display in one context (e.g. the classroom) and the understanding they display in another (e.g. the data-gathering situation).

These criticisms are clearly of some importance. If they were substantiated, then they would seriously undermine the specific methodological approaches adopted in this book. They would also seriously undermine our overall purpose of trying to generate empirically based models of progression in particular domains. Indeed, the 'situated cognition' argument can be seen as undermining one of the most fundamental purposes of schooling – that is, to generate understandings within pupils which can later be used in a wide (and unpredictable) range of settings outside of school.

The criticisms are, quite rightly, taken seriously by the various contributors to this book. Each set of authors addresses them either explicitly or implicitly in describing their particular methodological approach. Their responses fall into three main categories, although it should be noted that these categories are not mutually exclusive, and that any particular team can respond in more than one way.

One response is to argue that, while these criticisms exist, they are not considered to be of sufficient substance to warrant abandoning the whole enterprise. In other words, it is reasonable to operate on the assumption that children's understanding in a particular domain can, at some point at least, be described in terms of generalised concepts which can be applied in a range of different settings. In addition, it is also reasonable to make the assumption that tasks can be designed which provide some measure of the degree and extent of this understanding. This approach is explicitly adopted by Simon *et al.*, in Chapter 2, who note that

> We have worked on the basis that what the children say during the interview and what they do with the equipment we offer relate in some way to their cognitive constructs.

A second response is adopted by Leach *et al.*, in Chapter 5. Rather than merely justify their own approach, these authors consider alternative approaches which they might have used to throw light on their domain of study – pupils' understanding of the nature of science. For example, pupils could have been asked general questions about what they thought scientists do and why they do it; alternatively, pupils could have been observed while carrying out school science activities, and inferences made from these observations about their understanding of the nature of science. But as the authors point out, both these alternatives would have had their drawbacks. For example, pupils might differ considerably in how they interpret general questions about what scientists do. Alternatively, the understandings required for carrying out 'school science' may be very different from pupils' representations of the world which 'scientists' inhabit. Leach *et al.*, thus opted for a third approach, in which they presented pupils with tasks and questions specifically designed to elicit their understanding of the nature of science.

A third response is to regard the problem of generalised understanding as one which is essentially open to empirical investigation. In other words, one aim of research in this area might be to explore the extent to which there is consistency or coherence across children's performance on a range of different tasks. A further aim might be to examine the extent to which there is progression in this kind of consistency or coherence. This approach is explicitly adopted in Chapter 1 by Munn's study of literacy and numeracy in preschool children; she used a range of tasks to directly compare children's understanding both within and across these two areas. A similar approach is adopted by Simon et al., in Chapter 2, where they look at children's performance on a range of tasks within and across two different domains. Indeed, these authors explicitly argue that progression in mathematics and science could well be characterised in terms of an increasing widening of the contexts in which generalised concepts are applied. A similar position is adopted by Lee, Ashby & Dickinson in Chapter 3; in the course of their discussion of levels of understanding, they suggest that higher levels can be characterised by the ability to solve a wider range of problems and by greater explanatory power.

Clearly, these are issues of some complexity. Yet they are also of fundamental importance, both for understanding the nature of progression and for developing appropriate methods for studying it.

Five Studies of Progression

Having looked at some of the main methodological issues facing any study of progression, we now turn to examine more closely the five specific studies of progression whose findings are reported in this book. This section will present a brief overview of each study, while the next section will look at what has been learnt across all five.

The first study, described by Munn in Chapter 1, is concerned with progression in children's ideas about literacy and numeracy before they start formal instruction in these topics at school. Munn used a longitudinal design in which she followed 56 children during their last year in preschool. The children were seen individually once a term, and presented with a range of tasks and questions designed to elicit their understanding of literacy and numeracy. Munn reports clear progressions during this period in children's understanding in both areas. In the area of literacy, children became increasingly aware of the role that written text plays in reading a story; they also became more realistic about their own inability to read. In the area of numeracy, children became more competent in their use of counting, and in their use and understanding of written numerals. Munn found a significant relationship between the two areas of literacy and numeracy, in that children who were more advanced in one area were likely to be more advanced in the other, although this was not always the case. She also reports that, on entry to school, children were more advanced in their understanding of literacy than of numeracy; as she points out, this may reflect the fact that adults spend more time reading story books to young children than engaging them in activities involving number.

The second chapter, by Simon, Brown, Black & Blondel, is concerned with progression in learning mathematics and science. The authors studied children's understanding in two areas – measures and forces – between the ages of 6 and 13 years. As described earlier, this study used a mixed cross-sectional and longitudinal design. Separate groups of children in Years 2, 4, 6 and 8 were interviewed on two occasions a few months apart: during this period the children received a teaching input related to the topics being studied. The children were individually presented with simple practical tasks designed to test their understanding of specific concepts within measures and forces. Initial analysis of the measures data suggests that a number of clear progressions can be identified over this period – for example, in pupils' ability to measure the height of a model tower with a ruler, or in their ability to estimate such a height in metric units. However, there appeared to be little progression in other areas – such as their ability to estimate the height of a tower in non-standard units. Initial analysis of the forces data reveals a clear progression in pupils' ability to provide explanations of a situation where forces are acting in equilibrium; however, it is only at the most sophisticated level that pupils provide explanations which take account of the system as a whole. In both the measures and forces areas, the authors report wide variation between children within this age-range: as they make clear, some 6 year old children appear to be operating at a higher level than some 13 year olds.

The third study, by Lee, Ashby & Dickinson, is concerned with progression in children's ideas about history. The authors' concern is not so much with children's substantive knowledge of historical facts and information, but with their 'second order' concepts of historical enquiry and historical explanation. This study primarily used a cross-sectional design, although there was a small longitudinal extension. The main phase of the study involved over 300 pupils between 7 and 14 years, of whom over 120 were interviewed in depth: in addition, 96 children were video-taped working in groups of three. In the chapter, the authors describe a model of progression in children's ideas concerning historical evidence. The model, developed from earlier work, suggests that children's understanding may progress from a simplistic notion in which evidence provides 'direct access' to the past, to a sophisticated notion in which evidence is evaluated in terms of the inferences about the past which can be drawn from it. Lee, Ashby & Dickinson show how this model can be tested using data from tasks designed specifically for this purpose: the tasks described here concern the Roman occupation of Britain. Initial analyses suggest that their model is broadly supported by the data available. As in the previous chapter, the authors point to the wide variation in children's understanding: some of the 7 year olds in their study already have higher levels of understanding than some of the 14 year olds.

Chapter 4, by Millar, Gott, Lubben & Duggan, is concerned with progression in children's performance of investigative tasks in science. The authors argue that performance on such tasks involves both conceptual understanding of the domain being investigated and procedural understanding of the nature of scientific investigation, and they develop a model which involves both these types of understanding. Their model is illuminated by data collected from a cross-sectional study involving 80 groups of pupils (aged 9, 11 and 14 years). The pupils were, for instance, observed carrying out an investigation based around a cool bag used to keep a drink cool on a hot day; they were also questioned about their understanding of aspects of the investigation. Millar *et al.*, identify a number of important progressions underlying the groups' performance on the investigation: these include changes in the 'frame' used to conceptualise the task, changes in the pupils' understanding of thermal processes, and changes in the pupils' understanding of the notion of reliability. In conclusion, the authors argue that underpinning these changes is a more fundamental progression in pupils' understanding of the notion of empirical evidence in science.

The final chapter, by Leach, Driver, Millar & Scott, is concerned with progression in pupils' representations of the nature of science. The focus here is not so much on pupils' knowledge about particular areas of science (as in Chapter 2) or on their ability to carry out scientific investigations (as in Chapter 4); rather, it is on pupils' understanding of what sort of enterprise science is, what sorts of things scientists do, and how and why they do them. The chapter describes a cross-sectional study involving 90 pairs of pupils between the ages of 9 and 16 years. In the part of the study reported here, pupils were presented with various questions – such as 'How was the Earth made?' and 'Which is the best programme on TV?' – and asked whether these were the sorts of questions which scientists might study. Leach *et al.*, report clear progressions over this age range in several aspects of the pupils' responses: for example, the younger pupils were much less likely to refer to notions of empirical testability in their accounts of scientific activity. In conclusion, the authors argue that progression in such aspects of understanding the nature of science may be of direct relevance to progression in pupils' conceptual understanding of topics within school science.

Conclusions and Implications

The findings reported here constitute only a preliminary set of answers to the four questions posed earlier. More work is clearly needed before we can provide a full account of progression in any one domain, let alone across the ten subjects currently making up the National Curriculum in England and Wales. Some of this work will undoubtedly be done by the five projects featured here, as they carry out further analyses of their data-sets. Other work will have to await the funding of fresh projects. Nevertheless, we can still draw some tentative conclusions and implications from the work already carried out.

Most of the findings reported here bear directly on the first question, in that they are concerned with establishing some of the main changes in children's understanding within particular domains of learning. Thus, each of the five studies has been able to identify some clear progressions in their respective domains, either at the population or at the individual level. In itself, this is not too surprising: one would naturally expect to see significant developments in children's understanding as they become older and more knowledgeable. At the same time, these progressions in some areas of understanding need to be set alongside other areas identified here, where little or no progression has taken place. There are a number of possible explanations for such a lack of progression – including, for example, the fact that performance might be at ceiling or floor level, or the lack of specific teaching in the areas concerned – and we cannot at this stage state unequivocally which is the most appropriate. Nevertheless, it is clear that closer study of areas where progression does not occur could well increase our understanding of the areas where it does.

If we look more closely at the specific progressions identified here, they appear to take two main forms. On the one hand, there is evidence of learners becoming more knowledgeable within a particular domain: that is, they acquire an increasing number of domain-specific skills and concepts, and these become increasingly more organised and coherent. For example, the findings from Chapter 2 show a clear progression in children's conceptual understanding of measures and forces. On the other hand, there is also evidence of learners becoming more knowledgeable about the nature of the domain under study: thus there is progression in their notions of historical enquiry (Chapter 3), in their understanding of how evidence is used in science (Chapter 4) and in their wider conceptions of what scientists do (Chapter 5). At the preschool level we can see evidence for progression in both these kinds of knowledge: the children studied in Chapter 1 not only became more skilled within the domains of literacy and numeracy, but there was also progression in their conceptions of what it means to be literate (if not numerate). What is not clear from these studies – and must therefore constitute a focus for future work – is the relationship between these two types of knowledge: it is likely to be both complex and important.

The five studies also throw some light on the second of our four questions, concerning variation in individual levels of understanding. All five studies report considerable variation between children at any given age, with two studies (Chapters 2 and 3) specifically pointing out that some of their youngest children were already outperforming some of the oldest ones, even with a difference of some 6–7 years between the two groups. While such variation is not exactly unheard of, the size of the gap between the highest and lowest performers may still cause some surprise. It is also clear that the size of the gap is apparent at an early age: the findings from Chapter 1 show there is already considerable variation in children's understandings of literacy and numeracy when they start school at the age of five, and it is likely that this gap will widen as children progress through school. One further question raised by these findings – which again must be the focus of further research – is whether progression takes the same form in low-performing and high-performing children. In other words, are the low-performing children simply trailing behind the others, or are they on a different route altogether?

While the five project teams have provided some initial answers to the first two questions, they have so far paid less attention to answering the third and fourth questions (concerned, respectively, with progression in individual children, and with the effects of teaching). Yet already some insights are emerging from the two studies with a longitudinal element (Chapters 1 and 2) although both studies indicate that describing progression in individual children is likely to be a complex business: within the same individual, progress may be made in some areas, while others remain stationary or even show signs of regression. It also seems likely that the effects of teaching on progression will be hard to tease out, and will depend, amongst other things, on the detailed relationship between what is presented by the teacher and the level of understanding achieved by the learner. Nevertheless, both these questions are in principle open to careful empirical research, and their answers will be particularly valuable to practitioners.

It is clear from the preceding comments that much more work remains to be done before we have full answers to our four questions. Nevertheless, there are still a number of practical implications which can already be drawn from the work reported here.

First, the research has identified a number of specific areas where there appear to be significant gaps in children's understanding, and which could be given greater attention in the classroom. For example, Munn's findings in Chapter 1 suggest that preschool children receive relatively few experiences which alert them to the nature and function of numeracy (as compared to literacy); she suggests that this could be remedied by the greater use of activities (such as counting games) specifically designed for this purpose. A second example comes from the study of forces in equilibrium described in Chapter 2, where Simon *et al.*, report that relatively few pupils can provide adequate explanations in terms of the system as a whole; the authors suggest that this could be a suitable focus for teaching. A third example comes from Chapter 5, where Leach *et al.*, argue that pupils may misunderstand the purpose and nature of practical work in science, and that this may need explicitly pointing out to them (a similar point arises from the findings concerning 'frame' in Chapter 4).

Secondly, the research has already generated a number of conceptual frameworks, analyses and models of children's understanding in a range of different subject domains. These include the framework developed in Chapter 2 for studying children's conception of measure; the model developed in Chapter 3 for looking at children's understanding of historical evidence; and the model developed in Chapter 4 for considering the types of understanding involved when children carry out scientific investigations. From the research point of view, these models are primarily tools which assist in the collection and analysis of data. At the same time, they may well have a value for practitioners, in that they provide a framework which can be used for developing curriculum materials, for devising specific teaching activities, or for designing appropriate assessment activities.

Finally, the research reaffirms the belief that any curriculum and assessment system can – and should – be informed by carefully researched, empirical studies of progression in children's learning. As the work described here shows, this task is not simple; it will undoubtedly take some time. Yet as we write in 1995, the education system in England and Wales has just been promised a five-year period of stability, during which the most recent version of the National Curriculum will be introduced and tested out in schools. This five-year period represents an excellent opportunity to build on the work reported here and substantially increase our understanding of progression in the ten subjects of the National

Curriculum. Hopefully, we would then be in a position to ensure that any revisions made to the National Curriculum in five years' time would be based much more closely than they have been to date on a research-based understanding of progression in children's learning.

References

DES (Department of Education and Science) (1988) *National Curriculum Task Group on Assessment and Testing: A Report.* London: DES.
Donaldson, M. (1978) *Children's Minds.* London: Fontana.
Hughes, M. (ed.) (1994) *Perceptions of Teaching and Learning.* Clevedon: Multilingual Matters.
— (ed.) (1995) *Teaching and Learning in Changing Times.* Oxford: Blackwell.
Lave, J. (1988) *Cognition in Practice.* Cambridge: Cambridge University Press.

1 Progression in Learning Literacy and Numeracy in the Preschool

PENNY MUNN

Introduction

Children experience other people's reading for many years before they actually learn to read for themselves. From these early experiences they build up attitudes which are likely to structure their approach to reading, and their motivation to learn to read. Sulzby (1988) has described the developmental progression in early concepts of reading as a change from an oral story concept to a concept of reading as text based. Developmental progressions in numeracy are more problematic, since there appears to be an essential discontinuity between preschoolers' intuitive and unschooled understanding of quantity on the one hand (Fuson, 1988; Wynn, 1990) and on the other hand older children's understanding of the numeral system which we use to record and manipulate number (Carraher, Carraher & Schliemann, 1985; Hughes. 1986). While children appear to understand the use to which symbols are put in representing language long before they actually learn to decode such symbols, a parallel understanding of the way in which symbols are used in the representation of quantity does not appear to be in place early on in their development.

The study described here aimed to chart progressions in children's literacy and numeracy during the year before they entered school. The aim was to look at both literacy and numeracy in the same children, to see whether there were similarities across these two contexts in progressions in the children's understanding.

Methods

Fifty-six children from eight Scottish preschools were seen in their final year of nursery. The children were selected at random and the sample consisted of 31 boys and 25 girls. The mean age of the children was 46 months at the start of the study and 55 months in the June prior to school entry. The children were seen individually each term in order to investigate changes in their concepts.

The interview was constructed as an informal assessment of early literacy and numeracy skills and covered three broad areas:

1. *Storybook reading:*

   - Each child was invited to read from a beginning reader which contained a clear story in the pictures on the right-hand page, the full text of the story on the left-hand page, and a shortened version of the story beneath the picture.
   - Each child was read the story and then asked to read it again.
   - Each child was asked to point to where the story had been read from and to point to the words. Note was taken of whether children pointed to the picture or to the words in response to these requests.
   - Each child was asked whether s/he could read, when s/he would be able to read, who else s/he knew who could read and who had taught him/her to read.

Analysis of the book-related behaviour was used to categorise children's concepts of print and story. Analysis of what the children said about reading was used to categorise children's beliefs about themselves as readers.

2. *Counting and number words:*

   - Each child was asked to recite number words and to count a row of blocks. Note was taken of the extent of the children's knowledge of the numeral system.
   - Each child was asked to give a successively larger number of blocks. Note was taken of whether they used a 'counting' or 'grabbing' strategy in giving correct quantities.

3. *Recording quantity:*

   - Each child was asked to write down the quantity of blocks (1, 2, 3 and 4) in a set of four tins. Note was taken of whether the children used hieroglyphics, pictograms, tally marks or conventional numerals to do this.

- A secret addition was introduced and each child was asked to find the tin to which an extra block had been added (in all cases, this was the tin with two blocks, so the task for the child was to notice that their record of 'two' did not match the new quantity of three). The children were asked to justify their answers. Note was made of the role that the written record played in the children's solution of the problem and justification to the interviewer. The children's recording strategies were deemed to be functional (or literate) if they used their written record to infer the site of the secret addition.

Results

Reading

During the year there was a gradual fall in the numbers of children who thought they could read. Table 1.1 shows the numbers of children falling into each category of beliefs.

Table 1.1   Children's ideas about reading

	Numbers of children aware of text and believing they can read		
	Term 1	*Term 2*	*Term 3*
Aware of text	12	16	27
'I can read'	24	15	7

Progressively fewer children stated unequivocally that they could read as the year went on. Some of the children were adamant that they could not read, but a more common response was for the children to rationalise their lack of reading ability by reference to the immediate context. This produced a 'conflicted' category of 'I can't *really* read' or 'I can usually read but I can't read *this* book'. The most frequent response was to 'read' from the pictures and then to admit that this wasn't 'real' reading or to wait for a story to be read and then reread it from a mixture of memory and picture interpretation. Most of the children also made comments which highlighted their dependent status with regard to reading:

'My Mummy usually helps me.'
'At school, the teacher will read it first and then I can read it.'
'I can only read it to you if you read it to me first.'

Table 1.1 also shows the numbers of children who were aware of the role that the text played in the story (i.e. they pointed to the text when asked 'Where did I read that story from?'). There was a steady increase in these numbers. There was no association between text awareness and belief in ability to read, suggesting that the children's growing belief that they couldn't read was not necessarily *caused by* their awareness of text. Many of the children who were well aware of the role of text nevertheless had the confidence to use their memories and the pictures to tell the story. Many of these children were perfectly confident that what they were doing was 'reading', even though they were well aware that adults did things differently. This pattern of change shows how, as children's concepts of reading change, so their concepts of themselves as readers must also alter. It became clear that some of the children were articulating two definitions of reading. The first (and primary) definition was of reading as recounting a story from a book. The second definition, which developed later, was of reading as the interpretation of text. In terms of the children's subjectivity, this amounts to a transition from reader to non-reader and it was interesting to note the ways that the children managed this transition. Their explanations for their 'non-reader' status relied heavily on contextual factors (such as the book, the nursery setting, the absence of a parent) and also had a strong affective dimension. It was clear that the children's ownership of books, or of the people who told the stories, played an important role in their management of the cognitive conflict that accompanies the transition to the role of 'beginning reader' (Munn, 1994b). The children's identities as readers were thus linked to specific social and affective contexts.

Number

Table 1.2 shows the numbers of children who used counting as a strategy, the type of recording method they used, and whether or not the written record functioned as a memory aid in solving the secret addition. In this table, 'counters' were distinguished from 'grabbers' according to Wynn's (1990) definition, that is whether children actually counted blocks out (either silently or to themselves) when giving the interviewer a particular quantity, or whether they used a 'grabbing' strategy based on visual apprehension of quantity.

Table 1.2 Children's number strategies

| | Numbers of children using counting, numerals and a functional strategy | | |
	Term 1	Term 2	Term 3
Counters	12	26	31
Numeral users	6	17	24
Functional strategies	8	16	26

There were noticeable increases in the use of counting (rather than grabbing) as a strategy, the use of conventional numerals to record quantity, and the functionality of the children's written record. By the end of the year, around half the sample had begun to use conventional numerals to record quantity. The remaining children used either 'pretend writing' or they used pictograms or tally marks to depict the quantities. These iconic methods (pictograms or tally marks) incorporated the one-to-one correspondence of counting into the written record. It is noteworthy that nine of the children carried this correspondence over to their use of numerals in the early stages, recording '4' for instance as '1234' (see Munn, 1994a).

The majority of children who drew iconic records of the quantity to be remembered did not actually use these records in order to check quantities during the secret addition task. In other words, most of these iconic records were not functioning as written representations for the children, despite that fact that the quantity they represented was immediately visible. For the children who used numerals, on the other hand, these records invariably held (or rapidly developed) a function in this respect. The development of functional strategies for recording quantity was thus highly related to the children's use of numerals for making records. These strategies were both in turn highly related to the children's use of a counting strategy on the 'give a number' task. Counting strategies were therefore connected both with the use of numerals and with the strategy of referring back to a written record.

Most of the children believed that they had taught theselves to count. None of them mentioned help or support in counting, and many of them referred to it as a purely linguistic (rather than functional) activity. The majority of their references to the social contexts of counting involved counting games with friends or siblings, where the purpose of counting rarely appears to have been made explicit. Counting and number work were not generally seen by the children as a joint activity with adults, as an activity in which they might require help, or as an activity with a particular purpose

The relation between reading and number

Many children were showing very immature numeric strategies, even on school entry, while the number of children with few strategies for dealing with books and stories was quite small. Since both awareness of the function of text and the functionality of written records of quantity increased dramatically, it might be expected that it was the same children who were developing these ideas. Table 1.3 shows the association. This

Table 1.3 Relation between text and numeral awareness

	Non-functional recording	Functional recording
Little or no text awareness	11	8
Text awareness present	7	18

($\chi^2 = 3.9; p < 0.05; n = 44$ as 4 children were uncodeable and 8 were absent)

association was not large, however: Table 1.3 shows that some children who were not text-aware had functional written records and conversely that some children who were aware of the role of text did not produce functional written records. Numerals up to nine, being logographs (visual configurations which represent an entire concept), might be a particularly easy place for some children to begin their understanding of the nature of written recording.

The Nature of Progression and its Representation in Educational Processes

The longitudinal data presented here raise a number of points about the nature of progression in this early and crucial phase of learning. Certain methods of analysis (most notably, cross-sectional ones) tend to represent progression as asocial and linear. Such descriptions of developmental progressions often give the impression of a smooth and intrinsically motivated growth towards a point where children are finally ready to be taught particular things. This idealisation of the learning process produces accounts of progression which are not easily used by teachers, since they take no account of individuality in development. The assumption of linearity which is embedded in some descriptions of change tends to be accompanied by the following two tendencies in constructing curricula.

First, there is a tendency to construct progressions along curricular lines – i.e. to determine the various levels of complexity or abstractness and to assume that children will begin at what we see as the simplest level and then progress to the next hardest level, etc. While such curricular levels may be useful as a means of communication between teacher and pupil about the subject and the learning that is required, it does not necessarily follow that this is the actual route followed by children in the development of their understanding. Examples of this tendency sometimes occur in the teaching of arithmetic, where curricular progression may be determined by the level of complexity of the rules for manipulating symbols rather than by the level of conceptual difficulty of the procedures. Similarly, in reading, curricular progression may be determined by the presumed level of difficulty of the words contained in a text rather than by an analysis of the hierarchically organised processes involved in reading a particular text.

Secondly, there is a tendency to assume that the major progression in children's understanding in areas of symbolic activity such as reading and number consists of a shift away from understanding based on a concrete/verbal level of function to a written-symbol manipulation level of function. Sulzby's description of children's progressions in story concepts and Carraher, Carraher & Schliemann's analysis of unschooled children's numerical difficulties both share the assumption that children first learn a skill or a concept on the concrete level and then transfer the skill or concept to their (presumably newly developed) symbol-manipulation function. However, the longitudinal data presented here suggest that the relation between these two phases is far more complex than this, and that the concrete/verbal level of function develops alongside the symbol-manipulation function. This gives rise to the possibility that the two levels of function may interact with each other.

Evidence on Transitions and Social Influence

In this sample there was evidence that for some of the children development was proceeding on two co-existing levels (narrative and text; concrete correspondence and numeric symbol) before progressing from one level to another. Such co-existing levels may well represent transitional points which hold many clues about how to move children on to the next curricular level. For example, the children's iconic use of numerals incorporated their own counting actions into conventional symbols (1,2,3,4 – 4) thus providing a stepping stone from counting to numerals. Similarly, children's use of pictures and of their memory for narrative may support their initial attempts at decoding text. Accounts of progression should include particularly careful descriptions of such transitions, since they may hold an important role in the development of effective teaching strategies.

The pattern of results described here also points to the importance of the social context of children's symbol learning. A greater number of children had progressed to a spohisticated understanding of book reading than was the case with number. This may be attributed to the greater amount of time that adults spend reading storybooks to children in comparison to the amount of time they spend playing with numbers with them. It may also be attributed to the early developing adult goal-setting that occurs in storybook reading and the relative lack of goal-setting in numerical activities (Saxe, Guberman & Gearhart, 1987). This difference would relate particularly to the greater level of children's awareness of the functions of adult reading in comparison to their levels of awareness of adult mathematical activities.

Educational Implications

There are some implications for education in the preschool and early primary years which need further exploration. The first of these is that the usual practice of delaying the use of numerals until numbers are well comprehended is entirely supported. This practice could be further augmented by assessing the way in which children use numerals or other recording strategies, in order that the class teacher can acquire a fuller insight into the children's comprehension. The second implication is that children's understanding of the functions of text interacts with their use of numerals to some extent. Effective teaching and assessment of number understanding in the early years will require teachers to take children's understanding of print into account when assessing their understanding of number and numerals. The third implication (which requires further testing) is that the use of counting games to teach children the purpose and strategy of counting may have a lasting impact on children's entry into school mathematics by constructing a discourse of number. This discourse may have the effect of giving small children an idea of themselves as number-users, thus promoting their early entry into a culture of mathematics.

References

Carraher, T., Carraher, D. and Schliemann, A. (1985) Mathematics in the streets and in schools. *British Journal of Developmental Psychology* 3, 21–9.

Fuson, K. (1988) *Children's Counting and Concepts of Number*. New York: Springer-Verlag.

Hughes, M. (1986) *Children and Number*. Oxford: Blackwell.

Munn, P. (1994a) The early development of literacy and numeracy skills. *European Early Childhood Research Journal* 2, 5–18.

— (1994b) What counts as reading before school? Children's beliefs. In P. Owen and P. Pumfrey (eds) *Understanding, Encouraging and Assessing Reading: International Concerns*. London: Falmer Press.

Saxe, G., Guberman, S. and Gearhart, M. (1987) Social processes in early number development. *Society for Research in Child Development monograph*, serial no. 216, 52, no. 2.

Sulzby, E. (1988) A study of children's early reading development. In A. D. Pellegrini (ed.) *Psychological Bases for Early Education*. New York: Wiley.

Wynn, K. (1990) Children's understanding of counting. *Cognition* 36, 155–193.

2 Progression in Learning Mathematics and Science

SHIRLEY SIMON, MARGARET BROWN,
PAUL BLACK AND EZRA BLONDEL

Introduction

The Progression in Learning Mathematics and Science (PIMS) project has undertaken an investigation of progression in children's learning within linked areas of mathematics and science. Our aim has been to explore some of the issues underlying the ten-level sequence of the National Curriculum, in particular:

- whether a progression can be identified and described so that it matches children's observed learning patterns and helps diagnostic assessment
- the extent of invariance of progression in different children, and in children of different ages progressing at different rates
- the relation between progression in learning and the teaching experienced.

The notion of progression is clearly complex. In particular, each of the two areas, forces and measures, itself draws on several conceptual strands and a conceptual analysis can be used to define a model of progression. However, the relation between the logical/epistemological dependence of concepts as appreciated by the mature scientist/mathematician and the way children themselves begin to construct and link ideas is problematic. The role played by experience of school learning, in relation to any maturational limits, is not well understood. Part of the function of the project has been to try to identify some of the contributory features.

In order to explore the notion of progression on the short timescale that the project allowed, we chose to include both cross-sectional studies, using four age groups (years 2, 4, 6 and 8) and longitudinal studies over a limited timescale, observing changes which occurred over a 2/3-month period which included a teaching input related to the topic. The data include pre-test interviews, observations of teaching, and post-test interviews. These interviews have been carried out with two sets of six children (each from different schools) of four different age groups (years 2, 4, 6, and 8). Three primary and two secondary schools were included in the study. Each interview is of about 20 minutes in length, which transcribes to approximately ten pages. Each interview is a discourse between interviewer and child and the data to be analysed take the form of verbal responses, with additional notes about behaviours. At the time of writing (early 1995), the main body of data from interviews and observations is in the process of being analysed and written up.

The data are a rich source for analysis of children's learning, but the data reduction involved has taken longer than envisaged. In measures, an outline is appearing in which progression of each of four concept strands concerned with unit, length, scale and measures can be charted in relation to a development from purely rule-bound procedural performance through a mixed transition stage to a conceptually based performance which is more robust. In forces, strands related to predictions, vocabulary, word meanings, the nature of what is offered as explanations, and the identification of the entities acting, can be separated.

This chapter provides an overview of the research carried out in each area, and includes a sample of the results which are emerging.

Progression in Mathematics and Science Project: The Measure Aspect

Aim of this section

This section begins with a discussion of the nature of measure, which, together with specific research findings, provided a basis for the initial derivation of a conceptual framework for progression in measure. The test items in the empirical study are then described, and the methods of analysis used in the measure study. The final section discusses some aspects of progression, illustrated by some early findings.

A framework for measure

Explicit definitions of measure are very rare. Piaget, Inhelder & Szeminska (1960) suggest that:

> to measure is to take out of a whole one element, taken as a unit, and to transpose this unit on the remainder of a whole . . . measurement is

therefore a synthesis of subdivisions and change of position . . . the concept of measurement goes beyond the ability to carry out the necessary bodily movements . . . the ability to reconstruct a sequence of action comes much later than the ability to carry it out exactly. But secondly to be able to imagine movement is not enough, for the subject must link movement to reference point. (Piaget, Inhelder & Szeminska, 1960: 3)

This discussion highlights many of the contributory concepts in measure which were to form the basis of our framework, such as *unit, subdivision,* and *reference point,* although it is in effect only applicable in those cases in which physical repeatability of a unit is possible. In other sections of the same book Piaget, Inhelder & Szeminska note other important ideas, including *conservation* and *transitivity* (which we include in the *understanding of the property*) and *continuity.* These notions, together with related concepts of *number* and *number operations* (whole number, integer, rational, real, place value notation, equivalence, ratio, addition, subtraction, etc.) all underpin the measurement process.

Broadly, measurement of a quantity involves the construction of a homomorphism M from an 'empirical structure' (which will define a set of entities to be measured) on to the set of real numbers (Krantz *et al.,* 1971). The homomorphism must preserve ordering, and, where meaningful, zero, additivity and ratio. A measure is not generally unique, and different functions will define (or be defined by) different units of arbitrary size. *Sub-units and multiple units* can be defined in relation to the same way as unit to give a system of units.

The result of the measurement function can be represented on a number *scale,* which itself relies on a length measure (a linear functional relation between length and number). This gives length a pre-eminent position among measures.

Measurement scales can be regarded as *ordinal, interval* or *ratio,* depending on the properties of the quantity being measured. Ratio scales are associated with the measurement of quantities such as volume or weight, with repeatable units, meaningful zeros and ratios. (It makes sense, for instance, to talk about one volume or weight being twice as large as another.) Interval scales are those in which the zero is defined arbitrarily and there are no meaningful ratios, but there is additivity (linearity) and a sense in which the unit is of consistent size. Examples include the Celsius scale of temperature, or the time of day, in which the degree or the hour represent meaningful units; the gap between 3.00 and 5.00 (or even –5.00 and –3.00) on these scales is similar in some physical way to that between

5.00 and 7.00, although 6.00 is not twice as hot or twice as late as 3.00. Ordinal scales are those for properties such as IQ, or ice-skating competition score, with neither meaningful ratios nor consistent units (there is no meaningful sense in which equal intervals on the scale represent equal differences in performance), but which retain only the ordering of performance.

Although it would have been interesting to explore the differences between measures of different types in this study, to do so would have introduced too many variables and made the assessment too difficult for the younger pupils. Thus it was decided to focus only on physical properties with ratio scales, taking one with and one without a visual (extensive) quality. Length was selected as being familiar to young children and having a unique position with regard to the nature of scales, and weight because of the contrasting tactile perception, relative familiarity, and link with ideas of force.

Table 2.1 A framework for measure

Units	Number	Continuity	Linear Scale
intermediary	cardinal principle	infinity	linearity
arbitrariness	whole number	continuity	representation of units
reference point	place value		divisibility
unity	fraction		representation of divisibility
repeatedness	decimal		
non-standard units	addition		
sub-units	subtraction		
standard units	ratio		

The ideas of scale, number, units and continuity form the basis of the framework shown in Table 2.1. We have developed statements within these categories by offering activities to children, refining our ideas based on the children's responses, representing the refined activity to the same (and different) children and further refinement. The test items were influenced by the APU (DES, 1988) and CSMS (Hart, 1981) studies and the work of Piaget, Inhelder & Szeminska (1960). We also referred to Mathematics Teaching schemes such as Nuffield (Albany, 1983), HBJ (1991), SMILE (1993) and GAIM (1992).

Unit

The notion of unit is that one entity, defined physically (e.g. metre, kilogram) or abstractly (e.g. degrees celsius, kilometres per hour) can be used repeatedly and counted to find the size of a different quality, and that the size of the larger quantity is given as a ratio of the single entity and a label to denote the single entity chosen. That repeatable entity is a reference point and is called a unit. One of the features of established/official measurement systems is that the units used are standard, fixed and unalterable. In some measurement systems there are elaborate multiples and subdivisions (km, cm, mm) of standard units each with an accompanying label, but in others there is only one unit (temperature only has degrees). In the latter cases the subdivisions must be represented by fractions or decimals. To estimate successfully in a variety of contexts in standard units, children need to have an imagined size of the unit, and an understanding of the relationship between families of units and between units of the same family.

Number

Where there are no labelled subdivisions, parts of the whole must be described using decimals or fractions. In the metric system the divisions and subdivisions within any family are related to each other in a ratio of 1:10 (or a power of ten). An ability to use that ratio to change from one unit to a sub unit or from one unit to another within a family requires at least an implicit understanding of place value.

Continuity

Most, but not all, measurement systems share the feature that a quantity can be any size imaginable. Between any two points on a scale can be represented an infinite number of measurements. For example there are an infinite number of measurements between 31 cm and 32 cm but in giving a measurement between those two points we may say 31.2 cm, 31.26 cm, 31.263 cm, etc. What we read off a scale is always an approximation to the actual size. Most measurement systems are concerned with continuous quantities and so the issue of continuity and infinity underpin the conceptions and inferences of the act of measuring (albeit intuitively). Thus there are two sources of inaccuracy, the error of approximation and that of the measuring instrument.

Linear scale

The linear scale visually represents units, numbers, and continuous quantities. The scale uses the geometrical concept of length and the ideas built into number lines. One such idea is that of the cardinality principle: that the last number in the set is the size of the set. The scale, however, is more than a number line or counting rod: its arrangement reflects the notion of unit, divisions and subdivisions as well as the number/size. A scale can be graduated with lines and numbers. Units by themselves are reference points but the scale is the aggregation of the units, in a line.

The above framework assumes generality across all measurement systems with ratio scales. The work of Okano (1991), Gal'perin and Georgiev (1969) and Carpenter (1975) similarly treats measure as a body of knowledge in its own right, underpinning the process of measurement of a variety of physical properties (scalar quantities). Heibert (1984), Steffe (1975) and Hart (1981) on the other hand used the term 'measures' as synonymous with the collection of measurement processes in each of the separate domains specified by the scalar quantities.

This latter view is embedded in school mathematics where the specific skills of measurement of such quantities as length, area, volume, angle, weight and temperature, are taught, but with little emphasis on the underlying common concepts. For example, if pupils were asked to devise a measuring system for length, time or temperature that they could use if shipwrecked on a desert island, or to devise a measure of how good at mathematics they are, or of how well their teachers explain things, it is not clear that they would know what was required, let alone how to proceed. While expertise at measurement in the various domains is clearly very important, generalisation and abstraction across domains will both help retention of more specific knowledge, and demonstrate these processes which characterise the subject of mathematics.

Thus in our work we have focused on underlying general concepts within the area of measure. For the purpose of the empirical work these are situated in, but logically (although not psychologically) independent of, specific contexts within the specific domains of length and weight.

Much recent research into the learning of mathematics and science has demonstrated the lack of transfer of general procedures, and the situated nature of performance within each specific context (e.g. Lave, 1988). Clearly, if there is no commonality, there can be no conceptual understanding, thus denying both the generalised nature of the disciplines of mathematics and science, and the possibility of describing any progression in terms other than those of specific performance in specific contexts.

One of the hypotheses of the project to be tested is therefore that there are such general concepts which allow some description of progression in terms of conceptually based strategies. However, learning is clearly not of an 'all-or-nothing' type; progression in learning includes widening of the contexts with which ideas can be associated and deepening of the complexity of such situations, as well as beginning to make generalisations of a novel type. One of the outcomes of the project is to demonstrate the extent of any generalisation of application of the same concept in the same measurement domain but across different situations, and the same concept across different situations within different domains.

Evidence of such differences in children's understanding domains is given by Piaget, Inhelder & Szeminska (1960), Hughes (1979), Dickson, Brown & Gibson (1984) and Steffe (1975); in each case the researchers believe this difference in difficulty to depend on differences in the nature of what is being measured. Clearly, measures such as length and weight are conceptually easier than compound measures such as speed and density because, although perceptually there may be little difference, a full understanding of compound measures is dependent on an understanding of rate. Dickson, Brown & Gibson (1984) suggest that measurement of physical space such as for length, area, volume and angle are far easier than measurement of phenomena where the perceptual evidence is removed physically from the object being measured, as in weight, time and money. Furthermore an understanding of length is fundamental to any measurement system using a linear scale (Okano, 1991). An interesting study by Nunes, Light & Mason (1993) demonstrates the relative ease of measurement where the conventional measurement tool supports the perception of the dimension measured, as in the case of a ruler with length.

Test items

We have worked on the basis that what the children say during the interview and what they do with the equipment we offer relate in some way to their cognitive constructs. Thus two practical situations were offered: the *Towers activity* for length, comparing the heights of two towers and the distance between them, and the *Weights activity*, comparing the weights of two boxes. In each case a variety of different instruments were offered to help to elicit the underlying concepts the pupils had in relation to the framework shown earlier.

Tables 2.2 and 2.3 list the questions and our brief rationale for including each one, which relates it to the ideas in the framework.

Table 2.2 Towers activity

Question	Underlying concept interrogated
Which tower is taller? How can you find out? Can you show me how much taller this tower is than that one (using string)?	'Lead in' question Articulated use of intermediary Use of an intermediary (practice)
How tall do you think this tower is using duplo?	Use of non-standard units Estimation – imagined size of non-standard units Use of reference point
What did you think of to help you estimate?	Articulation of reference point
Can you tell me how much taller this one is using duplo?	Use of an intermediary
Let's find out how high it really is.	Physical repetition of units Understanding of number Recognition of outcome of measuring – number as result
Is it exactly . . . duplo?	Continuous variable Recognition of extra bits Understanding of number (fraction, place value)
If you had only one duplo how would you measure the height? (Show me)	Operational repetition of units
You seem to leave a space here/overlap here . . . will it make a difference to your answer? How?	Length as distance between two points Additiveness of measure
If you used duplo (larger unit) what would happen? Would you get more or less? Why?	Inverse relationship between size of units and outcome Arbitrariness of unit
What if you used a ruler? What would be the height of the tower? (Ask for a unit if its not offered.) What did you think of to help you estimate?	Estimation • use of reference point • imagined size (use) of standard unit

Table 2.2 *(continued)*

Question	Underlying concept interrogated
Let's find out using ruler (ask for unit).	Use of sub-units Using ruler as counting rod Length as distance between two points Using ruler as measuring instrument for continuous variable Recognition of extra bits
Is your answer exact? Can you ever get an exact answer?	Approximate nature of measure
What do you think is the distance between the towers?	Imagined size of standard unit
What did you think of to help you estimate?	Use of reference point
Let's find out using this ruler. Unit? Can you be more accurate?	Conversion from one unit to the next
What would make it more accurate?	Physical repetition of unit
Can you ever get it to be totally accurate?	Approximate nature of measure
What if you had used other side of the ruler (16ths)?	Arbitrariness of measure

Table 2.3 Weight activity

Questions	Underlying concepts
Which of these two is heavier?	Sensory relative direct pairwise comparison
How heavy do you think this one is?	Estimation – imagined size of unit
What can you think of to help you estimate the weight?	Use of reference point
Can you think of something which weighs the same?	Use of non-standard unit Imagined size of unit

Table 2.3 *(continued)*

Questions	Underlying concepts
How can you find out how heavy it really is using these ball bearings?	Use of multiples of a unit Additiveness of weight Number as result
Is it exact?	Infinity: number matched to degree of property Infinity: approximate nature of measure
What if we used a kitchen scale? How much do you think it would weigh?	Estimation – imagined size of g, kg, lb. Whole number of units Whole number and fraction Whole number and decimals
Let's find out. (Explore scale with metric and non-metric)	Reading of sub-divisions Sub-units
You said it was . . . kg. You used . . . ball bearings. Can you get it in kg using this balance? (two pans)	Arbitrary nature of measures
Let's use this digital scale. What do these numbers tell you?	Additiveness of weight Scale 1: many
Is the number exact?	Reading decimals off a scale
How could we get it to be more accurate? Can we ever be totally accurate?	Approximate nature of measure

Analysis

After going through the transcripts and accounts of pupils' actions we identified each aspect of pupils' behaviour which seemed to be significant in differentiating performance in measure in one or more of the seven different contexts (see Appendix 2). We devised a general coding sheet (see Appendix 1) which was applied to each context for each pupil, for both pre and post interviews. The data was then entered into a File Maker Pro data base.

Results and discussion

We are only just beginning to work on the data which is in the data base. In particular we have not yet started to examine the pre-test/post-test changes for the pupils, so that we have not yet any information that can be used to consider the third aim of the project relating progression to teaching. Nor have we been able yet to look at combinations of aspects to try to identify whether some of these link together to form more general categories of performance. We hope eventually to describe particular categories, either within each of the four strands of units, number, continuity and linear scale, or across these. Equally it may not be possible to do so.

However, results for individual entries in the coding sheet in each context are available and some of these are used to illustrate how we can begin to answer the first two aims of the project.

Identification of progression

It was obviously not expected that there would be any simple progression, in the sense that each aspect assessed would fall neatly into one of a set of progressive levels of difficulty, such that each student would have positive responses to all those below a particular level, and negative responses to those above.

If this were the case, the profile of the numbers of 'successful' pupils across the four year groups would follow one of a small number of patterns of rising lines, each pattern lying above the other so that none of them would cross (see Figure 2.1 for a set of behaviours which do in fact demonstrate this).

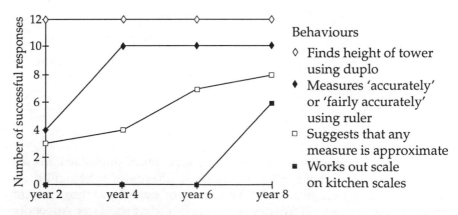

Behaviours

◊ Finds height of tower using duplo
♦ Measures 'accurately' or 'fairly accurately' using ruler
□ Suggests that any measure is approximate
■ Works out scale on kitchen scales

Figure 2.1 Results for a set of four behaviours which might suggest a sequence of progression (n = 12 for each age-group)

The four aspects shown in Figure 2.1 were selected to show a pattern which could theoretically suggest they might come from different 'levels' of understanding (although in the case of the three harder items there is no logical rationale for this). Not only should items from 'ideal' levels show this pattern, but the sets of 'successful' students for aspects in harder levels would have to be included in those for 'easier' levels, i.e. 'scalability'.

The three harder aspects above in fact are not perfectly scalable; for example, only two of the three Year 2 pupils who volunteer that their answers may be approximate, measure at least fairly accurately with a ruler. This is perhaps not surprising given that the tasks appear logically independent.

The question as to whether a progression can be identified depends on whether there are aspects which come near to fitting this model. We will be looking at the performances of the children across the aspects and at the aspects across the children in order to see whether we can identify one, or more than one, progression. Allowances have to be made for some error due to lack of reliability and validity in the 'items'. (The small size and unrepresentativeness of the sample will also need to be considered; any progression identified would clearly need to be tested on a larger and more representative sample.)

Table 2.4 Numbers of pupils (out of 12) in each age group demonstrating each of five behaviours

Behaviour	Year 2	Year 4	Year 6	Year 7/8
Estimates height of tower accurately (or fairly accurately) using duplos	6 (k, g)	9	7	7 (n)
Measures accurately or fairly accurately using a ruler	4 (k, g)	10	10	10 (not n)
Suggests that any measure is approximate	3 (k, g)	4	7	8 (not n)
Estimates weight of package using appropriate metric unit	2 (k, g)	0	2	7 (not n)
Estimates height of tower in appropriate metric unit	3 (k, g)	10	11	11 (n)

k, g, and n represent three pupils in the sample; the table indicates where they are included in the totals.

Nevertheless, it is immediately clear that some aspects would not fit easily into a progression. For example, as shown in the first row of Table 2.4, the results for the numbers of pupils who were able to estimate the height of the tower accurately or fairly accurately using duplo show a fairly flat profile suggesting that there is little progression between the four age groups. This is perhaps because it is a perceptual skill which is not dependent on knowledge other than counting. While this does not necessarily show that the item could not form part of a progression (for example if teaching it in Year 2 produced 100% response throughout then it could be at level 1 of some progression) it does suggest that given the current curriculum it is not appropriate.

Thus the gradients of the curves of performance are important when examining progression, even where the trend is generally upwards. For example, a rather odd profile is shown by the results of asking pupils to estimate the weight of a package which was about 250 g. The numbers who offered an appropriate metric unit (grams or kilograms), regardless of the accuracy of their estimate, gave the appearance of remaining low but random across the primary years with a steep jump into secondary (see the fourth row of Table 2.4).

This suggests that the result depended very much on previous experience of such units. The ability to associate the names of units to weights is very likely to be easily teachable at any of these ages, and is unlikely to offer much evidence of cognitive progression (although it is understandable that one might want to assess it at a particular point).

This type of associative learning may link with the use of scientific language, and historical knowledge as opposed to historical skills. Some regard the significant aspects of the curriculum as largely made up of such items, which could just as easily be included in the curriculum for any key stage. This leads us to the 'key stage' model for attainment targets proposed in the first Dearing report (Dearing, 1993) as an alternative to the ten-level model which presupposes some sense of progression in learning.

It will be important to examine changes in pupils' performance from pre- to post-teaching interviews in order to examine the nature of progression; this data will be analysed shortly.

It should be made clear in all this discussion that there can be no inference of *necessity*, logical or psychological, in our findings. If a particular progression is identified, this does not mean that this progression will hold for a larger sample, nor that it reflects any inherent sequence, either in the knowledge or in the pupils. We can only identify progressions which describe a particular group of pupils, with particular home circumstances and school curricula.

Relation to age

In the above discussion, the question of invariance of progression between different pupils was raised as part of 'scalability' of behaviours. Again we have not performed the detailed analysis on this but it is clear that there is some but by no means complete commonality. It seems possible that independent aspects will be identified which relate to one or more of the different strands in the framework.

It is clear, and not at all surprising, that some pupils perform consistently better than most of their peers, and some worse, and that at least some of these performances are common across the mathematics and science tasks. The results shown earlier are typical of a more general picture in that they suggest that for all but the very easiest or hardest tasks, there are some Year 2 pupils who demonstrate the behaviours, and some Year 7/8 pupils who do not, and on the whole that these are the same pupils across different tasks. For example, taking the aspects quoted in Table 2.4, it is clear that two Year 2 girls (k and g) outperform a Year 7/8 girl (n).

Thus it is fairly clear that not only in a single aspect but across a wide spread of aspects, some Year 2 pupils perform better than some Year 7/8 pupils. We still need to find out in which aspects the advanced Year 2 and Year 4 pupils differ from older pupils who have similar profiles of response.

Final note

Thus even with some limited results on single aspects, some important conclusions emerge about progression. When we have been able to look more widely across groups of aspects and groups of pupils we hope to have considerably more powerful conclusions.

Progression in Mathematics and Science Project: The Forces Aspect

Background

The development and use of test items to probe children's under-standing of forces has been reported more fully elsewhere (Black & Simon, 1992). This section provides a brief account of the test items and interview questions to set subsequent sections in context.

The test items

Three test situations were developed which enabled us to explore children's understanding of force in different contexts. These situations are referred to as 'Weight', 'Hanging box' and 'Bridge'. They are illustrated in Figure 2.2 and described as:

Weight: Children were provided with a 1 kg mass and different surfaces on which to push and pull it, including a table top, wood, and sandpaper.

Hanging box: Children were given a box attached to two elastic bands and a loop of string. The box contained a few stones and could be lifted by pulling up one band, two bands, or the string.

Bridge: Children were shown two bricks, a piece of thick card and a box containing a 400 g mass. A bridge was built with the bricks and card, and the box placed on the top. Other bridges were built using a thinner piece of card, and an identical box containing a 600 g mass. The lighter box could bend the thick card slightly and the thin card substantially. The heavier box made the thin card collapse.

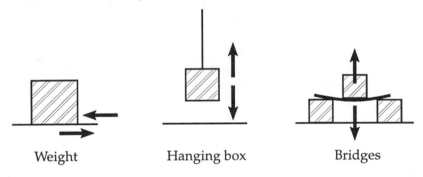

Weight   Hanging box   Bridges

Figure 2.2 The three tasks used in the interviews

The interview questions

Our approach was to design probes which originated both from the scientific understanding of the phenomena involving forces, and also from the simplest notions children have about these phenomena. For example, for the 'hanging box' we wanted to look for an understanding of the weight of the box as a downward force on the elastic, of the force upwards from the finger, of the forces in both directions from the stretched elastic, and of equilibrium. Our approach to this involved identifying what could be simple ways of perceiving and explaining the situation.

The interview begins with questions such as: 'What do you think will happen?' 'What do you see happening?'. These questions are followed by 'why?' questions to evoke explanation. To explore the notion of pushes and pulls, the next part of our probe is to see whether children identify source and direction of pushes and pulls in each situation. Children may identify these unsolicited, if they do not then specific questions are asked. The interview is then used to probe ideas of relative sizes of pushes and pulls, and notions of equilibrium. Children are asked about whether situations are balanced, and whether pushes and pulls in opposite directions (if identified previously) are the same or whether one is bigger than the other.

Thus, this interview schedule uses the three situations to explore children's predictions, observations and explanations of the phenomena in their own terms, and then to probe further specific ideas relating to scientific understanding. The interviews proceed according to the answers given by the children. Rather general open questions are followed by more specific and leading questions if natural follow up of the first responses does not cover some of the issues. If the child uses the terms 'force', 'gravity', or 'friction', then the interviewer pursues the meanings the child attaches to these terms. If the child does not mention these terms, then after all three items have been used to explore the child's own ideas, the interviewer probes for the child's understanding of these three and explores how he or she identifies them in each of the three situations.

Analysis

Our initial analysis involved coding and categorising a sample of the pre-test transcripts using systemic networks and open coding techniques (Bliss, Monk & Ogborn, 1983; Miles & Huberman, 1984; Strauss, 1987). The use of networks enabled us to organise the data into categories according to emphases within the interview design, so that key questions in the interview schedule elicited sets of responses that could be categorised together. Open coding of the data enabled us to take into account the nature and content of unsolicited responses, and progressively to focus on aspects of the data which appeared to have significance for progression in learning. Through combining these analytical methods we have devised a set of four major categories, or dimensions of progression, which have formed the framework for analysis of all the data. These dimensions are outlined below.

We have found that the interview responses are varied and diverse because children have different, often unique, ways of describing and explaining phenomena. The responses are also vague in many cases, and much cross-referencing between different parts of the transcript, to compare ideas expressed in the different test contexts, needs to be done to make inferences about children's ideas. To be authentic to the data and yet analyse the responses according to meaningful categories without simply repeating the transcripts is a complex task. It requires much re-reading of transcripts and cross-checking which has been very time consuming.

The four dimensions

By studying children's observations and explanations of phenomena involving forces we have conceptualised progression along four dimensions:

D1:   predictions and observations offered

D2:   identifications of pushes, pulls, force, friction and gravity

D3:   use of language in describing observations and in providing explanations, and meanings attached to words

D4:   nature and complexity of explanations.

D1: We get all sorts of predictions, for example some children think the elastic will break or the bridge will fall. Some children test out the cardboard of the bridge with their finger before giving an answer. Some children are reluctant to make predictions. The nature of the prediction (plus the need to feel the equipment) and the fact that predictions are richer for older children suggests that experience of phenomena is important. Linked with predictions are the observations and what they tell us about how children focus on the phenomena.

D2: An indication of children's knowledge of forces can be gained from how they identify push, pull, force and gravity in the test items. Data coded according to this category are statements which are either voluntarily expressed, or given as answers to direct questions.

D3: When presented with the test items children have to find words to express their observations and explanations. If we accept the view of social construction of knowledge through discourse then our study of learning must focus on children's use of language. The interviews with children consist of discourse about meanings and understandings, it is therefore essential to look at the data in the light of the vocabulary the children use. Also, in the forces domain we are particularly interested in how the use of language determines how children express meaning for force, friction, gravity, and how language relates to the acquisition of scientific understanding and enables children to explain distortion and equilibrium situations. Primary pupils have little experience of scientific terms, yet they have experience of cause and effect situations which they can describe and explain in their own terms, and such terms have to be interpreted carefully in order for us to understand a child's thinking.

Our analysis of the transcripts for use and meanings of words has focused on the key words and phrases children use to describe and explain the test items. We have also focused on how they respond to and use the terms force, friction and gravity. The key words, or derivations of them, are: rough, smooth, heavy, light, strong, weak, hold, stretch, bend, weight, balance, force, friction and gravity.

D4: This dimension focuses on the sorts of explanation children perceive to be appropriate and the nature of the explanations they offer. Some examples of questions for which responses have been coded within this category are:

- Why is sandpaper more difficult?
- Why is the elastic stretching?
- Why is the card bending?
- Why doesn't the box fall?

This dimension is discussed more fully in the results below.

Results

To show some of the results that are emerging from the analysis we include the section of the framework on equilibrium, with reference to the data for Years 2 and 6. We have focused on explanations in some detail, and indicate which aspects of the other three dimensions might be linked to these explanations.

Explanations relating to forces in equilibrium

To elicit children's explanations relating to situations where forces are in equilibrium, certain questions were asked for the items hanging box and bridge. Such situations occurred when the hanging box had been lifted and was hanging still (the elastic had stretched), and when a box had been put on the bridge and was supported by the bridge (the card had bent). Having talked about the box pulling or pushing down in each case, children were asked 'Why doesn't the box fall?' to see how they explained the balanced forces within the system. The responses were categorised as follows:

Hanging box:

1. Not asked
2. Don't know
3. Because it has stayed up (or similar)
4. It's being held/supported by hand/elastic/string
5. Lightness or lack of heaviness of box

6. Relative strength of elastic
7. Both 5 and 6

Bridge:

1. Not asked
2. Don't know
3. Because it has stayed up (or similar)
4. It's being held/supported by card/supports
5. Lightness or lack of heaviness of box
6. Relative strength/toughness/heaviness of card or supports
7. Both 5 and 6

The categories of explanations have been arranged in a hierarchy according to how, from a scientific point of view, they increase in complexity in terms of an understanding of the system:

- In category 3, children are simply saying that the box does not fall because it is staying up.
- In category 4 children are identifying an agent which is holding. Such an agent is the person, the elastic, the string or parts of the bridge, or the bridge as a whole. These explanations show no reference to properties within the system or forces within the system.
- In category 5 children refer to the lightness or lack of heaviness of the box, so they are focusing on one entity, that entity being the downward force associated with the box.
- In category 6 children refer to such entities as the strength of the card or the supports, so they are focusing again on one entity, but that entity is a materials property of one of the components; this may or may not imply a link of this property with existence of a force.
- In category 7 children mention both types of property, thus are explaining the situation with reference to the system as a whole.

Other, similar, hierarchies are emerging through analysis of other questions. One such question follows on from talking about why the box is not falling in the bridge situation. Children who do not mention the supports are asked 'Are the bricks [supports] doing anything?' to see how they explain the supports in the system. The answers can be categorised as follows:

- a description of the bricks (they are just normal like boxes)
- what the bricks are doing (holding)

- what the bricks are doing as part of the system (they help this thing not to go down off the cardboard by holding it up there)
- the system as a whole (holding the cardboard up – the box is going down and the cardboard's trying to go up to hold the weight of the box).

Categorising explanations in this way and constructing hierarchies of categories enables us to look at possible progression in terms of complexity of explanation, both across age ranges and for individual children. Tables 2.5(a) and (b) provide a sample of how this can be done. The pre- and post-test responses for the question 'Why doesn't the box fall?' are shown for the bridge item for Years 2 and 6. For example, in table 5.2(a) it can be seen that child b in Year 2 gave a simple response in the pre-test (category 3) followed by a category 6 response in the post-test. Category 1 (not asked) cannot be taken into account when looking at pre-to post-test changes.

Table 2.5 Grids to represent categories of each child in pre-test (vertical) and post-test (horizontal) dimensions for the bridge task with (a) Year 2 and (b) Year 6 children

(a) Bridge Year 2

Post / Pre	1	2, 3	4	5	6	7	Total
1			D	C, E			3
2, 3 c					b		2
4				f	e		2
5	B			d			2
6				F	A, a		3
7							0
Total 1	1	0	1	5	4	0	12

(b) Bridge Year 6

Post Pre	1	2, 3	4	5	6	7	Total
1							0
2, 3							0
4 Q			P, n				3
5		M		m		N, R	4
6 o				q	O		3
7				r		p	2
Total 2		1	2	3	1	3	12

Each table shows the change in response from pre- to post-test (three children c, o, and Q were not available for the post-test). Those on the diagonal line show no change. Those above it (top right) are children who have changed to a higher category, below are children who have changed to a lower category. For example in Year 2, children b, f and e have changed to a higher category, A, a, and d remain unchanged, and F has changed to a lower category. Shifts between categories from pre- to post-test are modest in both years, the most notable shift is child b who said he did not know (category 2) in the pre-test, yet when answering in the post-test gave a category 6 answer.

The tables can be used to show differences between years. For example 4/12 give category 6 answers in Year 2 post-test, 6/12 are in lower categories in Year 6 post-test. Many Year 2 children thus give higher category explanations than many Year 6 children. However the occurrence of category 7 explanations is absent in Year 2, whereas 4 children give such explanations in Year 6.

Discussion

The results we have so far in the explanations dimension raise some points worth noting:

- It is only at category 7 that we begin to see explanations relating to the system as a whole, with features interacting, and therefore to forces in equilibrium.
- Other work done in this area at secondary level (Clement *et al.*, 1987; Clement, Brown & Zietsman, 1989) begins at category 7, with an assumption that this is the starting point for teaching Newton's Third Law. There are much more elementary things that need to be teased out and explored for those (younger) children who do not explain what is happening in terms of the system as a whole.
- We are beginning to see the implications for teaching. For example, a useful teaching approach might be one in which teachers encourage children to discuss and explain situations by looking at the system as a whole, focusing on the interacting features of the system.
- The categories within our hierarchy are empirically based, yet the hierarchy itself has been constructed by our view of what constitutes a progression leading to an understanding of forces in equilibrium. The issue is whether this is a hierarchy in the sense of being a good guide to a learning sequence.

Our next step is to link results that are emerging from the analysis in the other three dimensions to these findings for explanations. For example, how do the same children predict and observe the phenomena, do their responses fall into similar categories? How do the children attach meaning to and use the words 'strength', 'balance' and 'force'? How do they identify pushes, pulls and forces (in answer to direct questions) in these situations? By examining the data in terms of these dimensions we hope to draw out the implications for teaching and learning, and develop teaching strategies for enhancing children's understanding of situations where forces are in equilibrium.

Appendix 1   Coding sheet used to analyse pupil interviews on measures

Units: estimation

Metric:	❏ kg	❏ g	❏ other	❏ appro	❏ inappro
Imperial:	❏ lb	❏ oz	❏ other	❏ appro	❏ inappro

Qualitative
comparison: ❏ correct   ❏ uncertain   ❏ incorrect   ❏ not made
Reference used: ❏ not asked ❏ not given ❏ ruler ❏ metre rule ❏ other
Accuracy: ❏ accurate ❏ fairly accurate ❏ given but way out ❏ not given
Label: ❏ volunteered   ❏ prompted   ❏ not given

Units: using instrument

Use of   ❏ volunteered ❏ use with help ❏ can use ❏ non-standard
instruments: use

Metric:	❏ kg	❏ g	❏ other	❏ appro	❏ inappro
Imperial:	❏ lb	❏ oz	❏ other	❏ appro	❏ inappro

Label: ❏ volunteered   ❏ prompted   ❏ not given
Accuracy: ❏ accurate ❏ fairly accurate ❏ given but way out ❏ not given
Aggregates: ❏ no   ❏ yes   ❏ successful   ❏ unsuccessful

Continuity

Whole number: ❏ only ❏ + a bit ❏ + half ❏ + other fraction ❏ + dec
Use of decimals: ❏ reads   ❏ understands   ❏ does not understand
Suggests about/in between/
a little more/less: ❏ never   ❏ sometimes   ❏ always
Number of values
in between: ❏ I can't tell ❏ none ❏ finite ❏ infinite ❏ see transcript
Is measure
ever accurate? ❏ not asked ❏ always ❏ never ❏ sometimes ❏ unsure
Because: ❏ instrument   ❏ technique   ❏ nature of measure

Relationships

Converts from: ❏ cm to cm ❏ cm to m ❏ cm to mm ❏ mm to cm
                        ❏ other   ❏ offered   ❏ prompted
            ❏ kg to g ❏ g to kg ❏ other ❏ offered ❏ prompted
            ❏ lb to oz ❏ oz to lb ❏ other ❏ offered ❏ prompted
Correctness of
conversion: ❏ always   ❏ sometimes   ❏ never
Using previously
found results: ❏ not applicable   ❏ yes   ❏ no

Appendix 1 *(continued)*

Conversion and
relative size: ❏ within metric   ❏ within imperial
            ❏ converts across both   ❏ acknowledges across both
Works out scale: ❏ trial and improvement   ❏ calculate
          ❏ 1:1   ❏ 1:many   ❏ 1:50   ❏ other
          ❏ successful   ❏ unsuccessful

Scale

Reads: ❏ off scale   ❏ by counting
Starts from: ❏ zero   ❏ elsewhere   ❏ not known

Appendix 2   The seven contexts used for the measures tasks

Duplo towers	accurate:	silver 14, pink 13½
	fairly accurate:	between 8 and 15
Ruler	accurate:	silver 27.5cm, pink 26.5 cm
	fairly accurate	between 25 cm and 30 cm
Measuring long distances	accurate:	1 metre + (different for each class)
	fairly accurate:	80 cm to 1 metre and a bit
Ball bearings on two pan balance	accurate:	9½
	fairly accurate:	between 6 and 12
Gramme weights on two pan balance	accurate:	249 g
	fairly accurate (estimation):	between 200 and 300 g
	fairly accurate (reading):	between 250 and 300 g
Kitchen scale	accurate:	249 g and 8.7 oz
	fairly accurate (estimation):	between 200 g and 300 g or between 8 oz and 1 lb
	fairly accurate (reading):	between 250 g and 300 g or between 8 oz and 10 oz
Digital scale	accurate:	249 g and 8.7 oz
	fairly accurate (estimation):	between 200 g and 300 g or between 8 oz and 9 oz
	fairly accurate (reading):	between 249 g and 250 g or between 8.6 oz and 8.7 oz

References

Albany, E. A. (ed.) (1983) *Nuffield Mathematics 5–11*. London: Longman.

Black, P. J. and Simon, S. A. (1992) Progression in learning science. *Research in Science Education* 22, 45–54.

Bliss, J., Monk, M., and Ogborn, J. (1983) *Qualitative Data Analysis*. London: Croom Helm.

Carpenter, T.P. (1975) The performance of first and second grade children in liquid conservation and measurement problems employing equivalence and order relations. In P. L. Steffe (ed.) *Research on Mathematical Thinking of Young Children* (pp.145–70). Reston, Virginia: National Council of Teachers of Mathematics.

Clement, J. with Brown, D., Camp, C., Kudukey, J., Minstrell, J., Palmer, D., Schultz, K., Shimabukuro, J., Steinberg, M. and Veneman, V. (1987) Overcoming students' misconceptions in physics: The role of anchoring intuitions and analogical validity. In J. Novak (ed.), *Proceedings 2nd International Seminar: Misconceptions and Educational Strategies in Science and Mathematics* Vol III (pp. 84–97). Ithaca, NW: Cornell University Press.

Clement, J., Brown, D. E. and Zietsman, A. (1989) Not all preconceptions are misconceptions: Finding 'anchoring conceptions' for grounding instruction on students' intuitions. *International Journal of Science Education* 11, 554–65.

Dearing, R. (1983) *The National Curriculum and its Assessment: Interim Report*. London: National Curriculum Council.

DES (Department of Education and Science) (1988) *Science at Age 11: A Review of APU Survey Findings 1980–94*. London: HMSO.

Dickson, L., Brown, M. and Gibson, O. (1984) *Children Learning Mathematics: A Teacher's Guide to Recent Research*. London: Holt Rinehart & Winston, for the Schools Council.

GAIM (Graded Assessment In Mathematics) (1992) London: Nelson.

Gal'perin, P. A. and Georgiev, L. S. (1969) The formation of elementary mathematical notions. In J. Kilpatrick and I. Wirszup (eds) *Soviet Studies in the Psychology of Learning and Teaching Mathematics* Vol 1. Stanford California: School Mathematics Study Groups.

Hart, K. (ed.) (1981) *Children's Understanding of Mathematics; 11–16*. London: John Murray.

HBJ Mathematics (1991) London: Harcourt Brace Jovanovich.

Heibert, J. (1984) Why do some children have trouble learning measurement concepts? *Arithmetic Teacher* 31 (7), 19–24.

Hughes, E. R. (1979) A comparative study of the order of acquisition of the concepts of weight, area and volume. *An Approach Through Mathematics and Science* (Chapters 8 and 10). London: Macmillan Education, Schools Council Research Studies.

Krantz, D. H., Luce, R. D., Suppes, P. and Tversky, A. (1971) *Foundations of Measurement*. New York: Academic Press.

Lave, J. (1988) *Cognition in Practice*. Cambridge: Cambridge University Press.

Miles, M. and Huberman, A. (1984) *Qualitative Data Analysis*. Beverley Hills: Sage Publications.

Nunes, T., Light, P. and Mason, J. (1993) Tools for thought: The measurement of length and area. *Learning and Instruction* 3 (1), 39–54.

Okano, L. T. (1991) The scale reading aspects of pupils' measurement performance. Unpublished Ph.D. thesis. London: University of London.

Piaget, J., Inhelder, B. and Szeminska, A. (1960) *The Child's Conception of Geometry.* London: Routledge & Kegan Paul.

SMILE (1993) *Secondary Mathematics Independent Learning Experience.* London: SMILE.

Steffe, P. L. (ed.) (1975) *Research on Mathematical Thinking of Young Children.* Reston, Virginia: National Council of Teachers of Mathematics.

Strauss, A. (1987) *Qualitative Analysis for Social Scientists.* Cambridge: Cambridge University Press.

3 Progression in Children's Ideas about History

PETER LEE, ROSALYN ASHBY AND ALARIC DICKINSON

Introduction

In recent years much interest and concern has been expressed by politicians and others about the purpose and quality of history teaching, levels of attainment and progression, and what it is realistic and appropriate to expect of children studying history between the ages of 7 and 14. In the UK there has been a contested redefinition of school history resting on a model which is explicitly constructivist, in which second-order structural concepts organise substantive knowledge and understanding, and in so doing provide the key to progression (both by defining the terms in which it takes place, and setting limits upon it). However, despite much interest in these issues in many countries, there exists little articulated theory with respect to the learning and teaching of history, and the empirical foundations of what does exist are not extensive.[1]

Research on children's thinking and understanding in history concentrated in the 1960s and 1970s on investigating children's understanding of substantive concepts such as *king*, *peasant*, *factory* and *revolution* (e.g. Charlton, 1952; Coltham, 1960; Wood, 1964; Hallam, 1967, 1975; Rees, 1976). The work was Piagetian in character, and approached history in much the same way as Inhelder & Piaget (e.g. 1958) approached children's thinking in natural science. This raised problems of methodology; whereas an experiment in *The Growth of Logical Thinking* provides (at least potentially) all the evidence required, if only the subjects use it, it is simply not possible in history to develop a test in which 'all the evidence is in'. In addition conceptual difficulties were raised about the nature and analysis of the concepts under investigation; there seemed to be no specifically second-order concepts, only notions borrowed from economics, politics or sociology.[2] A move to second-order ideas – to the investigation of children's

50

understanding of second-order concepts including evidence, cause, empathy and story and account – offered to solve some of these difficulties. It was also easier to see some structure in the development of children's ideas about second-order concepts, whereas their understanding of substantive concepts seemed to follow unpredictable paths mirroring both the complex interrelationships of such concepts and shifts in their meaning over time.

Similar changes were apparent in the teaching of history as well as research. The most important single driving force was the feeling that in studying history children ought to have to think as well as remember. This led teachers to look for ways in which history could be given a more rigorous structure, something that might provide a basis for progression in children's understanding of history, as opposed to the aggregation of historical facts, or the memorising of accounts. In a seminal publication, Shemilt (1980), probably the most influential figure in the development of the 'new' history, urged that adolescents should learn 'something of the logic of history and the meaning of such key ideas as "change", "development", "cause and effect" and so on'.

Second-order concepts such as *evidence* and *change* appeared to offer a way of picking out what was different about history, and here teachers and researchers began to share a common agenda. Researchers reacting against the Piagetian framework of investigation into children's thinking were increasingly treating history as *sui generis*, a very particular way of looking at the world which had to be properly taken into account if children's ideas were to be understood. Two distinct strands are discernible in this discipline-specific research. Some researchers (perhaps appropriately labelled post-Piagetians) moved away from the Piagetian paradigm, arguing against its mechanical application in history, but accepted its power and were reluctant to dismiss it in its entirety (e.g. Dickinson & Lee, 1978; Shemilt, 1980). Others (an anti-Piagetian tendency) attacked the whole Piagetian tradition as irrelevant to history, and claimed – perhaps not altogether convincingly – to have abandoned it completely (e.g. Booth, 1983, 1987).

In the mid-1980s these changes in history teaching and research influenced the reform of public examinations for 16 year olds (GCSE), and, despite opposition from some politicians and historians, have also influenced the attainment targets and the assessment system for history in the National Curriculum established in England, Wales and Northern Ireland as a result of the 1988 Education Reform Act. It is against this background that the CHATA project is proceeding.

The CHATA Project

The CHATA (Concepts of History and Teaching Approaches at Key Stages 2 and 3) Project is divided into three phases: investigation of the progression of children's ideas of *historical enquiry* and *historical explanation* between the ages of 7 and 14 years; the development of instruments for investigation of teaching approaches in history and for categorising the way in which history is seen in relation to the wider curriculum; and finally exploration of the relationship between pupils' concepts of enquiry and explanation, curriculum contexts and differences in teaching approach. This chapter will limit itself to a discussion of some issues involved in the first phase, for which data collection is complete, and analysis has recently begun.

CHATA builds on a continuing tradition of small-scale qualitative research carried out over a period of 15 years or so (e.g. Dickinson & Lee, 1984; Ashby & Lee, 1987; Cooper, 1991). The main aims of Phase 1 of the project are to test and refine provisional models of children's understandings derived from earlier work, and to develop new models where no adequate existing models are available. In order to do this CHATA is investigating a number of possible sub-strands in the concepts of enquiry and explanation, in particular evidence, accounts, rational understanding, cause and explanatory adequacy, and will examine the possibility of constructing models of progression for the wider over-arching concepts.

In the trial stage of Phase 1 the Project employed video and interview methods, together with pencil-and-paper tests. (Approximately 600 written responses were collected.) In the main investigation in Phase 1 pencil-and-paper responses have been collected from over 300 subjects between the ages of 7 and 14, across three batteries of tests. More than 120 of this main sample have been interviewed on all three batteries (on three separate occasions). Of these 120 subjects, just over 50 are 7 year olds, approximately 30 are 10 year olds, 20 are 11 year olds, and 20 are 14 year olds. In addition we have video data on 96 children working in groups of three, each group doing one battery of tests.

The test batteries themselves are designed to investigate children's ideas about historical enquiry and explanation in history. These over-arching concepts are sub-divided into five strands: evidence, accounts, cause, rational understanding and explanatory adequacy. (It is possible that we may also be able to say something about children's ideas of objectivity.) Each battery seeks to elicit children's ideas in a number of different ways, so that there is internal triangulation as well as triangulation across the three batteries.

We are now involved in the analysis of this data. As yet it is too early to say anything by way of conclusions, so this chapter will concentrate on some theoretical and methodological issues raised by the notion of progression in history in the context of models under development, give examples of test material employed, and discuss some illustrative responses.

Some Methodological Considerations

Researching history

There are important differences between investigating children's concepts in history and investigating their concepts in natural science. The subject-matter of history does not consist of experimentally manipulable objects, available to direct inspection. In history there is no apparatus to manipulate in front of researchers. (One point of such manipulation is in any case missing: history is not concerned with making general statements about the behaviour of physical objects.) This means that in history it is never possible to present children with all the evidence they require to arrive at the solution to some problem, even using everyday understandings. There is always a more or less arbitrary limit in what is put before children to enable them to show how they tackle a problem. Given that children approach the past with very different sets of experiences and expectations about what is humanly possible or likely, it is difficult to make secure decisions as to what subjects 'need to know'.

The written word acquires particular importance in history. Researchers have to strike a balance between risking incomprehension in the face of complex concepts, and simplifying to the point where subjects are denied certain cognitive moves by the constraints of the simplification. This is not a problem unique to history, but it has a particular importance in history, first because history is so dependent on linguistic manipulation, and second because teaching and research in history have turned their attention to second-order concepts. Pictures and objects do not alleviate the first problem, because subjects must, in Collingwood's words, look through them, not at them (Collingwood, 1946: 214). And because it is not possible to produce protocols of children's observable behaviour directly relevant to the investigation of their ideas, except the element of behaviour which is linguistic, it is hard to get at subjects' 'working', as opposed to their 'results'.

A problem with second-order concepts of the kind under investigation in CHATA (and which drive the National Curriculum assessment system in history) is that they are as much philosophical as historical concepts. As such they are likely to remain tacit, not in the usual weaker sense in which to say something is tacit is to say that it is not spoken or made explicit, but in a much stronger sense. Asking children direct questions about historical evidence, or even what they think about historical evidence, tends to produce responses which are very difficult to interpret; if the questions are about cause or rational understanding the results can be quite exotic. Under pressure to consider matters they have not only never confronted, but cannot even fit – as questions – into any meaningful context or human activity, children say what comes into their heads. It is hard to know whether such remarks are deeply significant or merely devices to maintain the confidence of the interviewer. Without an unjustifiably strong attachment to the psychopathology of everyday life, there is no way of reading off the status of the responses directly from the responses themselves. In any case, having a particular concept of cause does not entail being able to give an account of that concept. And assent to a proffered account, even where the account is an attempt to construct a valid representation of the subject's ideas from initial responses, and is offered by way of feedback, notoriously demands caution, particularly with younger children.

This forces the researcher back onto an indirect approach: perhaps it is possible to infer tacit ideas from the way in which children tackle historical tasks? A further difficulty immediately arises: how far are the skills demands imposed by the task distorting either the target understandings, or our access to them? There are several elements involved here, most of them too obvious to warrant mention, but the more interesting ones are linked to the concept of *level*, and will be pursued below. In any event, the indirect approach emphasises the hypothetical and conditional nature of any claims about children's ideas in this area. The best research of this kind can hope to achieve is an internally consistent system which is not disconfirmed by what children do. The expectation is that subjects will behave *as if it were true* that they believed certain ideas. This is not so fragile as it may seem; beliefs might arguably be subject to the same strategy as Alasdair MacIntyre (1958) employed in his definition of intention: 'the meaning of "intention" is elucidated by a categorical reference to behaviour supplemented by a hypothetical reference to avowals'. Whatever its conceptual underpinnings, however, this kind of constructivism is evidently high-risk in practice. There is no guarantee that children will have sets of ideas that are genuinely coherent, even with a notion of coherence of the kind that might be provided by a move like MacIntyre's. Over what range can we expect such ideas to be coherent?

The relationship between substantive content in history and the development of children's second-order 'structural' concepts is unclear, and no systematic work has yet appeared to shed any light on it. As already indicated, early attempts to find common routes taken by children from simple to sophisticated substantive ideas in history ran into difficulties: the concepts were interwoven in such complex ways, and children approached them from such different starting points that little progress was made in understanding substantive conceptual development in history.[3] The move to second-order concepts avoided the immediate problem only at the expense of creating another: how far do second-order ideas remain stable in the face of changes in substantive content? Our inability to answer this question is a strong reason for employing some form of triangulation across different substantive content in any attempt to acquire a better under-standing of children's second-order ideas about history.

Levels and progression

At this point it may be appropriate to make some simple remarks about some current conceptual schemes which provide a framework for handling progression in children's ideas and abilities. A central notion here is the idea of a level, which is (loosely) tied to the concept of progression. The minimal meaning of level allows for its use as a basis for assessment. Assessment levels are categories of achievements. A level is, on this reading, some convenient criterion-related category to which responses may be allocated. If it is to make sense a level should fit into a hierarchy of levels; the hierarchy may be single or multi-stranded, but it should normally stick to one of the two possibilities available for progression – understandings or skills. In research, by contrast, the idea of a level is related to theoretical and empirical studies of how children think, and imports its own set of assumptions.

This suggests an elementary distinction between two different types of categorisation, which might be called *assessment levels* and *construct levels*. There is obviously a degree of overlap here: in theory at any rate, levels of achievement should have some connection with what children actually do, and so there should be some relationship between the way children tend to behave – at least as suggested informally by evidence gathered from the examination performance of a wide range of candidates – and the levels system used to rank their performance. This informal evidence mirrors the more formal empirical warrant demanded by research, and in some cases examination evidence has proved invaluable in more formal investiga-tions. (This is true of examination work done in the Schools Council 'History 13 – 16' Project, for example, and the examinations for the new Cambridge History Project 16 – 19 follow-on course may prove similarly useful.)[4] Nevertheless, research clearly has its own purposes and standards which are not necessarily the same as those involved in examinations.

The notion of level as it is used in CHATA picks out something more than the minimal assessment notion. The hypothesis is that it is possible to find sets of tacit ideas that allow or inhibit certain cognitive moves. (Strictly speaking, of course, talk of 'finding' sets of ideas is misleading. Such a project is in fact doubly constructivist. In the first place it assumes that children operate with constructs which are more or less effective in handling the problems that 'history' throws up, where 'history' means whatever is perceived by them as history. In the second place the research attempts to construct a model of those constructs. The model is constructed and tested, not found: it is a postulate, not a discovery.) Children who handle history as though they believe that historical agents are more stupid than we are, but share our goals, beliefs and values, will run into severe difficulties in dealing with certain kinds of historical problem, or even in making sense of certain passages of history. An assumption that people in the past might see things in a different way from us overcomes the conflicts posed by the lower-level ideas, and opens up new possibilities for further conflicts at a higher level. Levels are higher or lower because they create or solve more or fewer problems, because the ideas with which children work can have greater or less explanatory power. In particular, higher-level ideas can resolve problems created by the limitations of lower-level ideas.

Triangulation on the basis of separate tests should enable us to say something about the persistence of ideas in the face of different content. But we have also attempted to design tests which each offer more than one kind of evidence about children's ideas. The hope was that we might be able to predict the level at which subjects respond to one form of question from knowledge of their response to another form. In particular, as well as requiring free-form responses, some tests require subjects to choose between statements, each of which represents a possible answer to the question at a particular level. If we can show consistency of level between free-form and statement-selection responses, we will have grounds for arguing for levels in the strong sense. This is a high-risk strategy: it will be quite surprising if we have succeeded in writing statements which subjects at a particular level select; and given that subjects were offered a range of responses to choose from, some of which are 'obviously' superior to others, it will be surprising if we are able to find any significant degree of consistency in their responses.

Underlying this strategy is the hypothesis that it may be possible to give sense to the notion of explanatory equilibrium at different levels, achieved through sets of tacit ideas. (Piagetian resonances of the notion of equilibrium would be amplified if it were to be interpreted by reference to field, mobility and stability, but there is no intention to import the full Piagetian theoretical apparatus here: merely to engage in some pragmatic borrowing.) The idea of an equilibrium is at least as important in its negative as in its positive mode. It is possible that at least two kinds of de-stabilisation occur. One form is when subjects (perhaps with increasing experience) see that their initial solutions to a problem leave questions unanswered, or actually create new ones. This may lead to the establishment of a new, higher-level equilibrium. The other form may occur when a task simply imposes too many demands. There is no reason here to expect a new equilibrium, merely, given less demanding tasks, a return to adequate functioning at the old one. In both cases, however, there appears to be the possibility of a more or less complete breakdown of the subject's normal procedures for handling the kind of problem in question. Attempts to solve the problem at a higher level, or to meet the demands imposed by task overload, can lead to responses at a very low level, with the apparent collapse of a range of understandings and skills outside those under test.

This sort of breakdown was apparent in early work on rational understanding; it also seemed to occur with A Level students working on the Cambridge History Project (see Lee, 1978; Dickinson & Lee, 1978). In the latter case it was particularly noticeable when students were attempting to evaluate a pair of tightly written, closely related, but clashing hypotheses, in the face of a body of evidence. The task of conceptualising the nature of the clash between the proffered hypotheses sometimes appeared to overwhelm the understanding that the sources could not be taken at face value: students who normally handled evidence *as* evidence lapsed into treating it as information, and fell back on matching strategies usually more common at Year 6. (It is not that such strategies are ever entirely absent in any cohort of A Level history students, merely that they are much less common.) Other examples occurred where students were handling taught distinctions between rational and causal explanation in the context of evaluating a proffered explanation; the normal historical subtleties dropped away, and (for example) specification of or distinctions between different groups were blurred into 'They did this', or 'People thought that'. If some concept of 'breakdown' is sustainable in the face of empirical evidence, it might offer a further reason for taking levels of the more ambitious kind seriously.

If our strategy fails, one reason might be that the notion of distinct levels is (at least) unworkable. It may be that the plethora of different strands of ideas cannot (either in principle or in practice) be woven into any relatively simple and robust scheme of levels. The basis for understanding progression may lie not in any particular set of levels, but in a multiplicity of alternative routes in the relevant concepts. And for some of these, we can hope to be able to claim to know something. Failure at this level should not mean that the research will have produced nothing of practical value. Clarification of children's ideas is valuable in itself, but, more immediately, even models which offer snapshots at more or less arbitrary moments in a process of change may have enormous heuristic importance. They can provide a clearer sense of what is at issue in addressing children's ideas in teaching, and offer a coherent basis for assessment. These would be acceptable payoffs.

Models of Progression in History

The construction of models of children's ideas is a task fraught with difficulties. How does one begin? Colleagues in science use anthropological analogies: researchers must cross the bridge from the country of adult practitioners to the land of child conceptions, and explore it, necessarily using the conceptual apparatus they have come to know and love in their own country. The problem is a very general one, and one with which historians are familiar from pursuing their ordinary business of trying to understand the past. It is too deep to be discussed properly here: we will simply make the assumption that it is possible to produce interpretations of other people's conceptual schemes, or parts of them, which allow their behaviour to be consistently interpreted, win some degree of assent from those who operate with those schemes, and even permit their behaviour to be treated as more or less predictable in the loose everyday sense. There is no scientific method (in the narrow sense) available at this point; the exercise is a hermeneutic one. Historians traditionally enjoin those who wish to make sense of the past to read in it until they know what the people they study will say next (Elton, 1967). Anthropologists live among their subjects with somewhat similar ambitions. The first steps for researchers into children's ideas are obvious enough: to work alongside children, to watch them, to set them tasks, to try to teach them and to see what children do with what is offered. Classroom teaching experience, small-scale piecemeal investigations using video-recordings, examination experience: all these can provide the first tentative ideas as to what will be fruitful ways of conceptualising children's assumptions.

Just as a historian must try to grasp the ideas of those under study, but is free to make sense of them in ways which go beyond their own framework, so research into children's ideas, while trying to say nothing false, may operate within a wider framework than the one subjects employ. But where research is investigating progression, there is also an irreducibly normative element involved. There is some notion of the higher levels of understanding of pre-existing concepts, and those concepts already carry with them and exemplify a structure. The structure, if accepted, sets out the internal differentiation and the boundaries of the area under study. So, investigating children's ideas about history, we try to construct a model of the development of ideas about evidence, and even as we do so it becomes clear that this is a proleptic use of the concept. We have split off an area of children's thinking about history on the basis of our conceptual schemes, not theirs. There is nothing illegitimate in starting with our own frame-work. The experience which children try to organise is already structured by adults on the basis of shared forms of life, and these forms of life are (to a great extent) available to children too. We have reason to believe that some conceptual schemes are more powerful than others: induction into these is part of what education is about. What is important is that, however we begin, we can show where children's structures differ from ours.

Similar issues apply at a smaller scale. If we start by investigating the development of children's ideas about evidence, we may soon find that such a progression ignores important internal structure: we should perhaps think in terms of other strands like context, questions asked, and testing. The trouble is that there is no reason to suppose that the structure is anything other than fractal: we can split strands into sub-strands indefinitely. But then who is to say what is a sub-strand as opposed to a strand? Why not start with children's notions of a historical question, rather than pull it out of their conception of historical evidence? In the end we must accept that, just as a historical reconstruction is in fact a construction, so any hermeneutic effort can only produce something justifiable, not the only interpretation.

Our initial models of children's ideas are therefore starting points derived from adult conceptions as modified by the experience of working with children. They are subject to adjustment in response to our data: where a model links ideas that do not seem to go together in subjects' responses, the model will be revised; where children make moves which are not available in the model, it will be extended; where children seem to be making distinctions which the internal structure of the model does not allow, new strands will be added; and if ideas held in one strand seem to predict those held in another, the model will be restructured in terms of the more predictive strand. But none of these adjustments will guarantee that the model is an accurate representation of children's ideas: merely that it is a workable construct.

Even as a workable construct a model may have only a limited shelf-life. It may be useful only under current conditions: for example, while teaching remains as it is, while examinations are set in present ways, and while children see history handled in roughly the way it is now in the media. There is unpublished evidence from follow-up studies of the Schools Council Project 'History 13–16' undertaken after the Evaluation Study which suggests that teaching substantially modified the way in which children's ideas on historical evidence developed. Any model produced by CHATA will be, in Shemilt's phrase, like sheep paths seen from high up: it will be the way most children happen to go at the moment; there will be no necessity in the progression.[5]

In Figure 3.1 the preliminary model of ideas on historical evidence, based on earlier small-scale video-recordings, is set out in Roman letters; the modifications suggested during trialling of the test materials are given in italics. The modifications are based only on informal analysis of the trials responses, and are offered here as no more than an example of ways in which the model might be modified and refined as we analyse the final Phase I data. The model is made up of statements about interlinked ideas, and while there is some reason to suppose that these ideas are indeed likely to be held in clusters of this kind, we cannot yet say with any real security what these are, let alone how strongly they are linked. The notion of a level here is one in which children operate with relatively stable sets of ideas, and those ideas are increasingly powerful from level to level. Children, for example, who have a concept of *evidence* can make sense of and use source material that would defeat pupils operating with a concept of *information*. At the information level children tend to regard conflicting sources with irritation: if they accept that there is a problem about what may safely be said, it is one which can be solved by counting the sources. If two sources agree and one is at odds with the others, the odd one is plainly wrong and the presence of two sources which say the same thing is simply a case of redundant material. Even at a testimony level pupils are convinced that historians are helpless in the absence of truthful eyewitnesses: it is only when they begin to acquire a concept of evidence that they understand that historians can use sources to answer questions which those sources were not designed, by a writer or maker, to answer.

Provisional Model of Evidence Levels

Level 1: Pictures of the past

The past treated as if it is the present; pupils treat potential evidence as if it offers direct access to the past.

Probably a useful category.

Questions about the basis of statements about the past do not arise, <u>nor is material questioned even as correct or incorrect information.</u>

Underlined passage probably incorrect: children operate with true/ false distinction, but it has no methodological basis.

Given statements to test against (potential) evidence, children are as likely to use the statement to knock out the evidence, as to use the evidence to knock out the statement.

Conflicts in potential evidence are not registered even as conflicts in information.

Too simple: material that threatens what children want to be true is noticed.

Level 2: Information

The past treated as fixed, finished and – by some authority – known; pupils treat potential evidence as information.

Broadly correct. Given statements to test against evidence, children match information, or count sources to solve the problem.

Questions arise about whether the information offered is correct or incorrect, but no methodology is attributed to history for answering such questions beyond an appeal to superior authority (bigger or better books, cleverer authors).

Satisfactory for documentary material, but ignores children's archae- ological knowledge. You can dig up things, and these give unmediated information. (You can even – in effect – dig up stories.)

Conflicts in (potential) evidence indicate incompetence on the part of the authors of books, or wilful awkwardness on the part of teachers.

Too simple: conflicts can arise because information is missing: no one has dug it up or read the right book. This may not just be incompetence: the book might have been lost, and no one knows where to dig.

Figure 3.1 Provisional model of evidence levels

Level 3: Testimony

The past reported either well or badly.

Questions as to how we know about the past are regarded as sensible: pupils begin to understand that history has a methodology for testing statements about the past. Conflicts in potential evidence are thought appropriately settled by deciding which **report** is best.

Notions of bias, exaggeration and loss of information in transmission supplement the simple dichotomy between truth-telling and lies. Reports are often treated as if the authors are more or less direct eyewitnesses: the more direct, the better.

Probably more or less satisfactory.

BUT:

As with previous levels, needs differentiation of sub-strands.

*For example, **plausibility** testing very evident here in the form of 'they would, wouldn't they', or, more sophisticated, 'How could she/he know?'*

But note that testing for plausibility against everyday assumptions as to what is possible occurs at the previous level.

Level 4: Scissors and Paste

The past can be probed even if no individual reporter gets it right: we can put together a version by picking out the true statements from different reports and putting them together.

In the words of one pupil to another: 'You take the best bits out of this one, and the best bits out of that one, and when you've got it up, you've got a picture.'

Notions of bias etc. are supplemented by questions about **whether the reporter is in a position to know;** it is not assumed that a report by an eyewitness is necessarily best, or that reports must be by witnesses.

Underlined passage may be misplaced: should be in next (higher) level?

*Plausibility testing is still of **reports**, but compares credentials of reporters.*

Figure 3.1 *(continued)*

Level 5: Evidence in isolation

Statements about the past can be inferred from pieces of evidence. **Evidence will bear questions for which it could not be testimony,** and many things may be evidence which are not reports of anything, and so historians may 'work out' historical facts even if no testimony survives. Evidence may be defective without questions of bias or lies – what weight it will bear depends on what questions we ask of it.

May appear earliest with physical objects (as opposed to written sources) . . . ??? We remain shamefully ignorant about children's handling of artefacts.

Pupils begin to understand that the overall picture constructed on the basis of evidence by the historian may itself be turned back upon the evidence to evaluate that evidence. (Evidence does not provide fixed points unless we choose to make them so.)

*Almost certainly misplaced. Should be indicator of next level. But needs investigation: often hard to distinguish between this **reflexivity** and simple appeal to everyday plausibility.*

Level 6: Evidence in context

Evidence can be made to do the sort of work picked out in the previous level only if it is understood in its historical context: **we must know what it is meant as, and how it relates to the society which produced it.**

This involves the suspension of certain lines of questioning, and a provisional acceptance of much **historical work** as established fact (a known context). We cannot question everything at once.

Contexts vary with place and time (a sense of period begins to be important).

At the moment this seems a reasonable shot at which ideas make the difference. Our current work only deals with pupils up to Year 9 (14 year olds), so it is harder to refine this.

But Cambridge History Project work suggests higher levels:
especially ideas about the way different kinds of claims relate to evidence.

Figure 3.1 *(continued)*

Examples of Tests and Responses

The examples used in this chapter are taken from the first battery of tests. As with the other batteries, enough substantive material was presented to the children to allow them to tackle questions on individual progression strands within an overall theme which provided the content of a self-contained unit. The theme of the first battery was the invasion and occupation of Britain by the Romans, and their subsequent withdrawal.

Evidence

The provisional model given above provided a working hypothesis. The Cambridge History Project (a course following on from the Schools History Project, and intended for 16 to 19 year olds) provided further insight into how to construct a test which might expose children's ideas for handling evidence and interpretation. Test materials would need to include at least two claims which had a relationship with the sources provided, together with a coherent set of sources that, if treated in certain ways, showed that they were regarded as information rather than evidence, creating tension or conflict if treated merely as information, but allowing such conflicts to be resolved if taken as evidence. This approach maintained a clear relationship between a claim to knowledge and the grounds on which it rests. Designing these tasks is extremely difficult if they are to reveal the understanding of pupils who may operate with a very wide set of ideas. These difficulties are exacerbated if the same materials are to be used on pupils ranging from 7 year olds to 14 year olds.

The evidence material used by 10–14 year olds is shown in Figure 3.2. The three stories relate to the six sources in different ways. (For 7 year olds the volume of test material was greatly reduced, and only two stories were offered.) Story B relates to the sources used as evidence and accounts for, and explains, all six sources. Story A lends itself to the total weight of the written sources treated as collective information, including somewhat implausible claims. Story C's claim rests on the visual, active sources of Arthur as a hero in the middle ages. Story C also provides its own rationale for its claims and appears powerful on the basis of length and detail. The children were asked to choose the story they thought was best according to the clues, to provide a reason for their choice, and to say which clues were helpful or unhelpful in making this choice. They were then asked to consider why somebody else might choose the other stories. (Examples used here are from Year 9 responses.)

People who are interested in the past sometimes argue about whether something is true or not. Below are three stories from three different books.

READ THE STORIES CAREFULLY

Story A:
About the year 500 there lived a very brave king of the Britons called Arthur. He fought the Saxons and won all his battles. In his twelfth battle at Mount Badon he killed 960 Saxons himself.

Story B:
About the year 500 a leader of the Britons fought the Saxon invaders and defeated them several times. One of his battles was at Badon Hill. He became a hero.

Story C:
About the year 500 there lived a King called Arthur. Arthur and his knights fought a big battle at Mount Badon. Arthur wore heavy armour with a picture of Mary, mother of Jesus, on it. This helped to make him very brave when he rode into battle. At the battle he killed many Saxons.

Sometimes we have CLUES to help us to decide how true a story is. We have some clues about this story.

STUDY THE CLUES CAREFULLY

Clue 1: Written in 540 by a British Monk called Gildas
Some Britons were murdered by the Saxons, some were made slaves. Some fought back under a leader called Ambrosius. Sometimes the Britons won the battles and sometimes the Saxons won. There was a big battle at Badon Hill. I know about this because I was born in the year it happened.

Clue 2: Written in 800 by a Welsh Monk called Nennius
The war leader was called Arthur. His twelfth battle was on Mount Badon. At the battle Arthur killed 960 Saxons all on his own. He won all the battles he fought.

Figure 3.2 Evidence material used by 10–14 year olds

Clue 3: Written in 1125 by a Monk called William
At the battle of Mount Badon, Arthur killed 900 Saxons all on his own.
He had a picture of Mary, mother of Jesus, on his armour.

Clue 4: A painting done in 1400 showing King Arthur killing Mordred.

Clue 5: A picture of King Arthur and his knights fighting the Saxons, drawn about 1400.

Figure 3.2 *(continued)*

Clue 6: A drawing of a soldier of the 400s and 500s (based on finds dug up by archaeologists).

Figure 3.2 *(continued)*

Children make a variety of recognisable moves in handling what their teachers call 'evidence'. For some subjects making decisions about historical claims is a matching exercise. Details from a story are picked out and matched to corresponding details in the clues to confirm a choice that may already have been made quite irrespective of the clues. For example, story A is chosen because:

> Clue 2 says that Arthers 12th battle was at Mount Baden and that is what it said in the Story A. Also in clue 2 he killed 960 Anglo Saxons on his own – so does story A. Everything in clue 2 matched story A.

Clue 2 was most important in helping to decide story A

> because everything in clue 2 matched story A.

Clues 4, 5 and 6 didn't help at all

> because they did not have the information I needed.

For some subjects, the story or claim takes precedence over the clues, which only have a place if they support the chosen story. In the following example, story C is chosen because I think that it was the most accurate.

Clue 3 was most important in helping to decide

> because the clue is the most accurate to the story.

There were clues that didn't help at all

> because I chose the story and the clue 3 had the most information I needed but the other two did not give me any information to the story I chose.

It seems natural to regard the following extract as an indication that the subject is treating the historian's problem as one of handling information. The subject offers as reasons for choosing Story A that:

> There are a lot of facts. It tells you when it happened, who he fought, he had won all his battles, it was his 12th battle and where it was and how many he killed . . . Clue 2 also contains facts that agree with those in story A. Clue 5 shows what the scene was like . . . Clue 3 doesn't have any real facts apart from saying that he had Mary on his armour. Clue 4 just shows Arthur killing someone.

There is an awareness here of the seductive nature of detail. The subject suggests that some people will have chosen story C

> because it provides them with details such as what he was wearing. Maybe they think that the person who wrote it knew what he was talking about because he gave them details.

This even suggests that this subject is aware of how persuasive detailed information can be in validating itself.

Other characteristic moves might be regarded as a sign that the problem is seen as one of finding reliable testimony. The subject in the next example argued that Clues 6 and 1 were most important in helping to decide

> because they were both based on things that happened soon after or around the time of the battle. How can someone, 1000 years after the battle know what the battle scene looked like? that is why I disregarded clues 2, 3, 4, 5.

However, the response suggests that this is still a very limited under-standing of the idea of testimony. Clues 2, 3, 4 and 5 didn't help at all

> because they were written ages after it happened and were probably lies, all lies and the authors probably didn't have a clue and just felt like being creative . . . I do believe it is important that things are believed only if the person who wrote/drew it was alive or saw it when it happened.

Other subjects recognise the importance of testimony but go beyond this to consider it in relation to other available evidence, and some even operate with a notion of disconfirmation. Another move is to treat coherence as adding weight to testimony, making it 'more likely'. Sources are then treated as a set rather than being picked off one at a time as isolated voices from the past. Context becomes important. Story B

> fits in best with clue l, the story that was written by someone who lived in the era. Because of this it is more likely to be correct . . . clue 6 helped me to eliminate clue 3 and so also story C because this mentions him wearing heavy armour which was not used at the time.

This reference to context is very clear in the following response to a question asking how one might decide whether it was likely that Arthur had a picture of Mary, Mother of Jesus, on his armour (as suggested by Clue 3):

> By finding out wether Arthur was religious and by finding out if Arthur wore Armour or not.

Children's responses are often complex, and any attempt to categorise a subject's response must obviously take the whole picture into account. Subject 91 chose story B because: 'it fitted the clue that wasn't exaggerated, written by a monk in 540, who was alive at the time. Both the other stories were exaggerated.' This response would fit the provisional model at Level 3: Testimony. This seems confirmed by his 'Clue 1 helped me the most because it was written by a British monk who lived at the time this happened and he obviously is not biased in anyway as he is not putting down either the Britons or the Saxons.' He goes further than this in explaining: 'All the clues were helpful, even if they were biased. They show that he did become a hero as they all show him killing or winning fights or tell the tale of how great he was.' He appears to be clear that story B can account for all the clues and whether they are biased is not the issue – they still need to be accounted for, and are, in story B. In considering why some people might have chosen Story A, the subject claims 'some people may have chosen Story A because more of the clues agree with story A than story B'. As he recognises that matching details is a move someone might make, this choice must have been available to him but rejected. He follows this by saying 'Story A makes him sound a hero which is exactly what some people want to believe'. His next sentence makes it clear that he is able to see how the clues can relate differently to the different stories 'People might choose story C because this has lots of information, most of which is included in the clues'. Taken as a whole subject 91's response appears to go beyond Level 3: Testimony; he rejects the matching of information as a possible move, recognises that bias does not make potential evidence useless, and so is able to accommodate a wide range of sources within a claim by his choice of Story B.

Subject 92 chose story A: 'because all three written clues say Arthur himself killed 900–960 Saxons as story A says.' The written clues also say this was at Badon Hill which also complies with Story A.' He matches information without reference to its validity other than that of numerical weight. There is no attempt to consider the likelihood or plausibility of this claim. He explains: that 'Clues 1, 2, 3 and 5 were helpful because they all agree (apart from 4) that Arthur fought against the Saxons, whilst 4 shows no sign of Mary on Arthur's armour.' Validity is again identified by numerical weight and what the eye can or cannot see. His response seems to fall within the Information category of Level 2, but there may be an element of Level 1: Pictures of the Past, operating here in his dealings with picture sources. This seems confirmed when he follows this by saying: 'Clue 6 did not help at all because it does not show anything about Arthur'. In responding to the question that asked why someone might have chosen the other stories he suggests: 'Some people might have chosen story B because it mentions an English leader fighting the Saxons at Badon Hill. Some people might have chosen Story C because it mentions Arthur and the fact that there was a fight at Badon Hill.' This attributes the same tactics to others' choices as the one he used in his, matching specific items of information. What something 'mentions' is obviously important to him. Perhaps his choice did rest on some notion of numerical weight even though he is wrong in claiming that all three written clues say Arthur himself killed 900 – 960 Saxons. Source 1 does not mention any specific number. It may be that he was including story A in 'all three written clues'.

Both these pupils responded to the question: 'Clue 2 tells us that Arthur killed 960 Saxons. How would you decide whether this was true?' Subject 91 wrote: 'Is it possible for a man to kill 960 men in one battle. I believe it is impossible so I decided it is not true.' Subject 92 wrote: 'By looking at primary sources and by finding out the number of people in the battle.' The subject has perhaps been taught about primary sources but does not have a workable understanding of what these can do. His use of the term does not help him. There is no sign of understanding of what might count as a test for a claim of this kind. Subject 91 on the other hand is clear about how he would decide.

Subject 93 chose story C 'because it has a lot of detail and description in it. Also I have heard it before. Clues 1, 2 and 3 helped best because some of the facts in the clues were in Story C. Clues 4, 5 and 6, didn't help at all because the pictures didn't really show any facts or figures.' The meaning of the word 'fact' to this subject is something that can be picked out in a very particular sort of way, not anything that actually needs to be established or validated. He makes no distinction between clues 4, 5 and 6. They are all just pictures, so the distinction that he makes between facts in the written clues and the absence of facts in the picture clues, does not take account of the type of picture clues he has available.

Subject 94's response highlights the difficulties faced in the trialling stage. 'I chose story A because I like the story of King Arthur and I watch as many as possible on TV so I believe A. None of the clues helped me. Clues 1–6 weren't helpful at all.' Trialling the tests had revealed that children chose between the stories for a variety of reasons. These reasons did not necessarily include a consideration of the validity of a claim in relation to the sources, but solely on the basis of internal dimensions, or the internal power of a story in relation to the internal power of competing stories. Some of these ideas are of course more powerful than others, but are still limited in connection with understandings about evidence. At least one interviewee explicitly asked to be allowed to decide on a story first before looking at the sources. Asked for a rationale particular children who took this path responded by saying things like: 'It is the most like the story I know already'; 'I've seen it on television'; 'I like it because it tells me about how brave Arthur was'; 'It has lots of details like names and dates and numbers so it must be right'; 'because it's longer, so it must be better than the others'; 'because it's shorter and more straightforward'. These were not all merely low level responses to the task: some responses asserted 'this story explains more than the other'. Where responses like this were followed by testing against sources for validity, it was possible to see very high level ideas operating. The test had to take account of, and identify, those children who made their initial choices in this way, i.e. before taking the sources into account. Initial trials suggested certain possible categories for each story in connection with this type of response and the test offered children a box containing statements which they could use to justify their choice, by underlining from the given list a reason that was most near their own. Three different lists had to be provided to fit the choice of story as it was clear that each of the three stories produced its own range of reasons for being preferable to the other two.

Systematic analysis has only just begun so it is difficult (not to say unwise) to try to offer anything more at this stage. Initial forays in the stacks of responses suggest that the revised model does provide a basis for children's sets of ideas about evidence but that further adjustments will need to be made to that model and refinements developed within the levels.

Cause

Several different approaches were used to elicit ideas about cause. Three of these will be illustrated (open questions, cause boxes and conflicting explanations) by reference to items from one battery of tests. (The other batteries used logically similar items, but different content.) Historical material sufficient to enable children to form a judgement on why the Romans were able to conquer Britain was given to the children: it covered background information on Rome and Britain, and the events of the Roman conquest. The question presented to the children took the form of a paradox:

There were lots of Britons in Britain.

The Roman army that went to Britain wasn't very big.

The Britons were fighting for their homes.

SO WHY WERE THE ROMANS ABLE TO TAKE OVER MOST OF BRITAIN?

This was asked first in the form of an open question, for which children had to write a few lines in answer. (The immediately following questions will not be dealt with here: one was designed to ascertain whether children distinguished reasons for action – why the Romans invaded Britain – from causal factors contributing to Roman success; and others were intended to shed light on children's ideas of conditionship and the generalisability of causal explanations.)

The children were then asked to draw arrows linking boxes to show why a cup broke: this was partly a device to familiarise them with a certain kind of exercise – the apparent abandonment of history at this point was accounted for in these terms – and partly a means of seeking evidence about their everyday causal notions. The boxes contained short sentences which might have some bearing on the breaking of the cup: some described events ('The cup hit the floor'), some referred to states of affairs ('The floor was hard'), and some described actions ('Jane and Fred both tried to grab the cup'). There were six boxes in all that might be used in the explanation. (The question is reproduced in full in Appendix 1.)

The next question asked the children to do the same thing in order to give the best explanation they could of why the Romans were able to take over most of Britain. This time the six boxes contained statements about the Roman Empire or about the Britons. (See Appendix 2.) In both the cup and the Roman take-over questions, children were told that an arrow from one box to another meant that the first box helped explain the second, and that they could have as many or as few arrows as they needed. They were also told that more than one arrow could go into or out of a box.

In the third approach, two different – very brief – explanations were offered to the children. One set out two simple background conditions for Roman success, and the other offered an event which was both a key step in the Roman conquest, and an immediate cause of their success:

The Romans were <u>really</u> able to take over most of Britain because the Roman Empire was rich and properly looked after.	The Romans were <u>really</u> able to take over most of Britain because they beat the Britons at the battle by the River Medway.

Subjects were then asked: 'How there can be two different explanations of the *same* thing?' Subsequent questions asked whether one explanation was better than the other, how they could check to see if one was better than the other, and how they could check to find out if either explanation was a good or bad explanation.

One part of the rationale behind these questions is an attempt to discover whether there is any kind of depth-structure in children's handling of causal explanation. Some children simply give haphazard lists of causal factors in answer to the open question, and then in the box-questions make a few single joins to the centre box which has to be explained. They behave as if causes are discrete and additive. Others give a narrative of events in the open question, and then narrativise the box-question. Typically this consists in producing a linear sequence which may encompass all the cause-boxes, or just some of them. There appears to be a range of ideas operating here, with some children treating processes and states of affairs as if they were events, and others using a narrativisation strategy but showing some awareness of the different status of the connections they make. At interview children using a narrativising strategy will talk in terms of 'beginning here', and use 'and then' or 'and next' as link expressions. On rare occasions spontaneously, and sometimes under pressure from the interviewer, some subjects will pause in dismay when they see – during the course of explaining to the interviewer what they have done – that one box does not make another happen, but precedes it, or is part of a pattern of joint causes. Finally, some children construct a causal argument in answering the open question, and then use arrows to produce what can only be described as an analytical schema for the box-question. Background conditions are picked out as separate starting points for different, sometimes separate and sometimes interlinked, causal chains which lead into the events for which they are conditions. Actions and events are often treated separately from background conditions. Sophisticated ideas of causal structure seem to be operating here. (See Appendices 3, 4 and 5 for examples of different strategies – 3 and 4 are from Year 9 responses, and 5 from a Year 7 response.)

Early work on the responses to the box-questions indicates that talk of levels in this area may not be entirely misplaced. A preliminary consistency analysis based on a crude tripartite categorisation suggests a very high degree of consistency in the strategies adopted by subjects in the face of different historical content. (One-sample Chi-square test for goodness of fit against frequencies expected by chance, significant beyond the 0.001 level for each year-group, as well as the group taken as a whole.) In the least consistent group (Year 7) some responses showed interesting signs of changing strategies while working on one task: for example, the deletion of a narrative pattern and the substitution of an analytical alternative. Analysis of responses to other questions will allow us to develop more sophisticated understandings in this area.

The question based on the two alternative explanations sheds light on children's ideas about causal structure and about the status of causes. Some children will only allow one explanation to be correct, others will accept both, but treat them as interchangeable and discrete. Some children decide that adding the two explanations together will give a better explanation, but still others argue that one makes the other happen, or even, taking a more sophisticated line, is necessary for the other. They insist that both explanations are valid, but treat them as exhibiting a structure which means they cannot merely be added to one another, and are not interchangeable: one child characterised them as 'direct' and 'indirect' causes. Few children have any strategy for testing an explanation except by checking that the statements in it were true; for most, a cause is epistemologically speaking on a level with a statement of fact, and is either something that happened or existed, or is not. Nevertheless some children (usually able 14 year olds) suggest counter-factual thought experiments, and even comparisons with similar phenomena in different times or places as a means of evaluating explanations.

If further analysis confirms that there is progression along the lines outlined above, it is important not to assume that it is tied directly to age. From our (limited) preliminary analysis, it is clear that some 7 year olds perform at a higher level than some 14 year olds on at least some of the tasks. (The PIMS Project has similar large variations in children's under-standing of key concepts in mathematics and science: see Chapter 2, this volume.) These findings raise important questions for theorists (What accounts for the variation?); for policy-makers (How can a national curriculum take account of it?); and for practitioners (How can it be dealt with in the classroom?).

During the course of analysis that now needs to be done we will attempt to develop, test and refine our crude picture of children's understandings of cause and explanation, evidence and the other strands we have picked out. We hope eventually to arrive at a model which identifies consistent strategies pursued by children, suggests relatively stable sets of ideas, and allows the characterisation of progression in these ideas in terms of their increasing power and scope. We will investigate the relationship between different strands, and perhaps be able to comment on the possibility of speaking meaningfully about progression in the over-arching concepts of enquiry and explanation, as well as in specific more narrowly conceived strands. These are goals which we may not achieve, but any moves towards them will help us to develop a workable concept of progression in history which can serve as a basis for assessment, a diagnostic tool for teachers, and a means of addressing pupils' ideas as directly and effectively as possible.

Notes

1. Early work in this field has, with two exceptions, used small scale samples. The two exceptions are the evaluation of the Schools Council History 13–16 Project (Shemilt, 1980) and the present CHATA Project, funded from 1991 to 1995 by the Economic and Social Research Council.
2. This way of putting things begs important questions; politics, for example, is arguably best understood as history, social science and philosophy. It also ignores the temporal extension and shifting meaning of concepts used in history, and the relation between concepts and historical particulars.
3. Coltham(1960) (for example) grappled with pupils' substantive ideas, and was more successful than most, but this whole research programme almost completely ground to a halt in the mid-1970s. It is now beginning to be revived: Hilary Cooper's work with primary children (1991), and the research of Maria Do Ceu Melo, currently in progress in Portugal, both partly deal with substantive concepts.
4. A great deal of work in connection with the Schools Council Project 'History 13–16' was done after the formal Evaluation Study, and involved longitudinal studies (unpublished), together with more informal evaluation of examination response patterns, some of which is hinted at in the reports of the Southern Regional Examinations Board. See the reports of the SREB in the late 1970s and early 1980s, Shemilt (1980). See also Shemilt (1983, 1984, 1987).
5. The analogy of sheep-paths is from private discussion with Denis Shemilt. Our own guess is that the paths for second-order concepts are relatively constant in comparison with those for substantive concepts partly because of the high level of generality of second-order concepts, and partly because they are not issues which children have had to think about, or in connection with which they have encountered interventionist moves from teachers. As this changes, models may have to change too.

Appendix 1   This question is to help you do the one on the next page. Do this one first.

WHY DID THE CUP BREAK?

HOW TO DO THIS QUESTION
Choose any boxes which help explain why the cup broke.
Join them up to show in the best way you can why the cup broke.
(The boxes are not in any special order)
Make the best explanation you can. Draw in arrows to make the joins.
An arrow from one box to another means: the first box helps to explain the second box.

Like this: This box   helps explain   this box.
Use as many joins as you need. You can have more than one arrow to or from a box.
BUT don't make joins that don't help explain why the cup broke.
Make the middle box happen!

SHOW WHY THE CUP BROKE

The cup was
made of china.

BOX 1

The floor
was hard.

BOX 4

The cup was
very breakable.

BOX 2

SO: THE CUP
BROKE.

Explain this box.

Jane and Fred
both tried to
grab the cup.

BOX 5

The cup hit
the floor.

BOX 3

Jane and Fred
dropped the
cup.

BOX 6

Appendix 2 Why were the Romans able to take over?

(The boxes on this chart are not in any special order)
Choose any boxes which help explain why the Romans were able to take over.
Join them up with arrows to show most clearly why the Romans were able to take over.

An arrow from one box to another means: the first box helps explain the second box.
Use as many joins as you need. You can have more than one arrow to or from a box.
BUT don't make joins that don't help explain why the Romans were able to take over.

Make the middle box happen!

The Roman Empire was very rich.

BOX 1

Roman armies were made up of full-time soldiers. They were well trained and were given good weapons and armour.

BOX 4

The Roman Empire was kept in order and looked after properly. The Emperor's orders were obeyed.

BOX 2

SO:
THE ROMANS WERE ABLE TO TAKE OVER MOST OF BRITAIN.

Explain this box.

Second clash. After the two smaller battles, the Romans beat the main army of Britons at a great battle by the River Medway.

BOX 5

The Britons did not all have the same leader. They lived in separate groups each with its own leader. Some Britons hated other Britons more than they hated the Romans.

BOX 3

First clash. Soon after the Romans landed, the Britons attacked then with two separate armies. The Romans beat each army one at a time.

BOX 6

Appendix 3 Why were the Romans able to take over?

(The boxes on this chart are not in any special order)
Choose any boxes which help explain why the Romans were able to take over.
<u>Join them up with arrows to show most clearly why the Romans were able to take over.</u>

An arrow from one box to another means: <u>the first box helps explain the second box.</u>
Use as many joins as you need. You can have more than one arrow to or from a box.
BUT don't make joins that don't help explain why the Romans were able to take over.

Make the middle box happen!

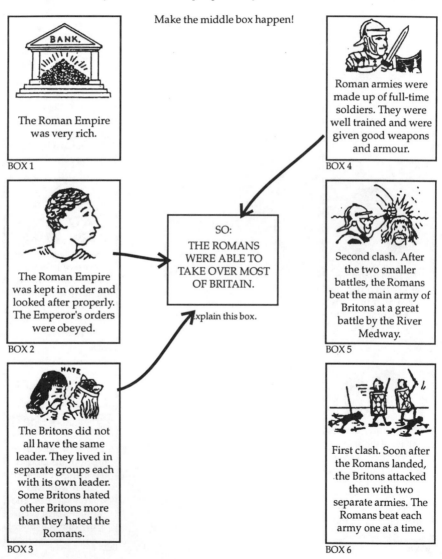

The Roman Empire
was very rich.

BOX 1

Roman armies were
made up of full-time
soldiers. They were
well trained and were
given good weapons
and armour.

BOX 4

The Roman Empire
was kept in order and
looked after properly.
The Emperor's orders
were obeyed.

BOX 2

SO:
THE ROMANS
WERE ABLE TO
TAKE OVER MOST
OF BRITAIN.

explain this box.

Second clash. After
the two smaller
battles, the Romans
beat the main army of
Britons at a great
battle by the River
Medway.

BOX 5

The Britons did not
all have the same
leader. They lived in
separate groups each
with its own leader.
Some Britons hated
other Britons more
than they hated the
Romans.

BOX 3

First clash. Soon after
the Romans landed,
the Britons attacked
then with two
separate armies. The
Romans beat each
army one at a time.

BOX 6

Appendix 4   Why were the Romans able to take over?

(The boxes on this chart are not in any special order)
Choose any boxes which help explain why the Romans were able to take over.
Join them up with arrows to show most clearly why the Romans were able to take over.

An arrow from one box to another means: the first box helps explain the second box.
Use as many joins as you need. You can have more than one arrow to or from a box.
BUT don't make joins that don't help explain why the Romans were able to take over.

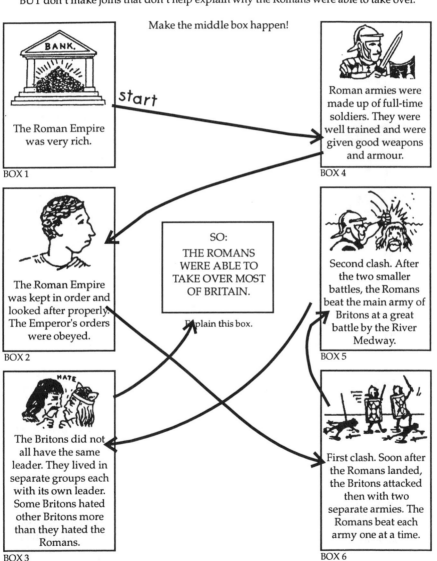

Make the middle box happen!

start

The Roman Empire was very rich.

BOX 1

Roman armies were made up of full-time soldiers. They were well trained and were given good weapons and armour.

BOX 4

The Roman Empire was kept in order and looked after properly. The Emperor's orders were obeyed.

BOX 2

SO:
THE ROMANS WERE ABLE TO TAKE OVER MOST OF BRITAIN.

Explain this box.

Second clash. After the two smaller battles, the Romans beat the main army of Britons at a great battle by the River Medway.

BOX 5

The Britons did not all have the same leader. They lived in separate groups each with its own leader. Some Britons hated other Britons more than they hated the Romans.

BOX 3

First clash. Soon after the Romans landed, the Britons attacked then with two separate armies. The Romans beat each army one at a time.

BOX 6

Appendix 5   Why were the Romans able to take over?

(The boxes on this chart are not in any special order)
Choose any boxes which help explain why the Romans were able to take over.
<u>Join them up with arrows to show most clearly why the Romans were able to take over.</u>

An arrow from one box to another means: <u>the first box helps explain the second box.</u>
Use as many joins as you need. You can have more than one arrow to or from a box.
BUT don't make joins that don't help explain why the Romans were able to take over.

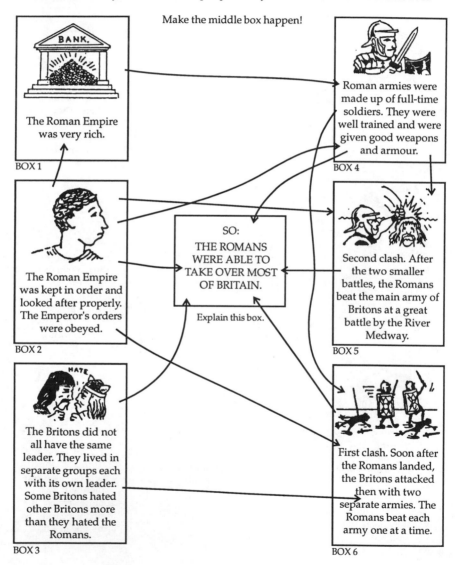

References

Ashby, R. and Lee, P. J. (1987) Children's concepts of empathy and understanding in history. In C. Portal (ed.) *The History Curriculum for Teachers*. Basingstoke: Falmer Press.

Booth, M. B. (1983) Skills, concepts and abilities: The development of adolescent children's historical thinking. *History and Theory*. Beiheft 22: Middletown, Weslyan University Press.

— (1987) Ages and concepts: A critique of the Piagetian approach to history teaching. In C. Portal (ed.) *The History Curriculum for Teachers*. Basingstoke: Falmer Press.

Charlton, K. (1952) Comprehension of historical terms. Unpublished B.Ed. thesis, University of Glasgow.

Collingwood, R.G. (1946) *The Idea of History*. Oxford: Oxford University Press.

Coltham, J. (1960) Junior school children's understanding of historical terms. Unpublished Ph.D. thesis, University of Manchester.

Cooper, H. (1991) Young children's understanding in history. Unpublished Ph.D. thesis, University of London.

Dickinson, A. K. and Lee, P. J. (1978) Understanding and research. In A. K. Dickinson and P. J. Lee (eds) *History Teaching and Historical Understanding*. London: Heinemann Educational.

— (1984) Making sense of history. In A. K. Dickinson, P. J. Lee and P. J. Rogers (eds) *Learning History*. London: Heinemann Educational.

Elton, G. R. (1967) *The Practice of History*. Sydney: Sydney University Press.

Hallam, R. N. (1967) Logical thinking in history. *Educational Review*, 19.

— (1970) Piaget and thinking in history. In M.Ballard (ed.) *New Movements in the Study and Teaching of History*. London: Temple Smith.

— (1975) A study of the effect of teaching method on the growth of logical thought, with special reference to the teaching of history using criteria from Piaget's theory of cognitive development. Unpublished Ph.D. thesis, University of Leeds.

Inhelder, B. and Piaget, J. (1958) *The Growth of Logical Thinking*. London: Routledge & Kegan Paul.

Lee, P. J. (1978) Explanation and understanding in history. In A. K. Dickinson and P. J. Lee (eds) *History Teaching and Historical Understanding*. London: Heinemann Educational.

MacIntyre, A. C. (1958) *The Unconscious, A Conceptual Analysis*. London: Routledge & Kegan Paul.

Rees, A. (1976) Teaching strategies for the assessment and development of thinking skills in history. Unpublished M.Phil. thesis, University of London.

Shemilt, D. (1980) *History 13–16 Evaluation Study*. Edinburgh: Holmes McDougall.

— (1983) The Devil's locomotive. *History and Theory* XXII, 4, Middletown, Wesleyan University Press.

— (1984) Beauty and the philosopher. In A. K. Dickinson, P. J. Lee and P. J. Rogers (eds) *Learning History*. London: Heinemann Educational.

— (1987) Adolescent ideas about evidence and methodology in history. In C. Portal (ed.) *The History Curriculum for Teachers*. Basingstoke: Falmer Press.

Wood, D. M. (1964) Some concepts of social relations in childhood and adolescence investigated by means of the analysis of definitions. Unpublished M.Ed. thesis, Nottingham.

4 Children's Performance of Investigative Tasks in Science: A Framework for Considering Progression

ROBIN MILLAR, RICHARD GOTT,
FRED LUBBEN AND SANDRA DUGGAN

Introduction

The Procedural and Conceptual Knowledge in Science (PACKS) project is concerned with the responses of children aged 9 to 14 to given science investigation tasks. Investigations, as a component of science teaching and learning, have grown in prominence in recent years in the UK and are now established as a major element of school science within the National Curriculum model (DES, 1989, 1991). While there is widespread agreement among science teachers and educators that developing the ability to carry out a scientific investigation is an important part of learning science, there is no established tradition of teaching or assessing investigation perform-ance. As a result, National Curriculum Attainment Target Sc1 Scientific Investigation has caused considerable difficulty for many teachers and has stimulated more discussion and criticism than most other aspects of the Science National Curriculum.

The focus of interest in the PACKS project is on the understandings which underpin children's performances in response to investigation tasks. We are interested in the interplay between children's understanding of the science facts, ideas and concepts which are relevant to a given investigation (sometimes referred to as *conceptual knowledge*), their understanding of the procedures of scientific investigating (*procedural knowledge*), and the details of their actual task performance. The aim of the project is to develop and validate a model relating aspects of understanding to elements of performance. (For a fuller account of the background, methods and analysis framework used in the project, see Millar *et al.*, 1994.) Such a model would allow us to begin to characterise more precisely the nature and extent of the differences between 'novice' and 'expert' performance in investigating in science. That is, it would provide the ground for a model of progression in performance.

This chapter begins by exploring some general issues associated with the idea of progression. It then relates these to the particular domain of interest to the PACKS project, and proposes a model linking understanding and performance. Data from the project are then used to illustrate differences in performance in relation to this model. The chapter ends with some general comments about the nature of progression in performing science investigations.

The Practical Importance of a Model of Progression

Some notion of progression, either implicit or explicit, underpins all teaching, and all syllabus and course construction and assessment. Consider the 'history' of an individual child's experience of a school subject, such as science. She or he will experience a sequence of science activities, either embedded in topics or explicitly separated out as 'science lessons', planned by a series of teachers. The teacher provides some experience or activity for the child in each lesson or 'time slot'; the child experiences activities and events in a time-sequence. The choice for the teacher (or for whoever plans the programme of instruction) is not between *having* and *not having* a model of progression; it is between having an *implicit* one or one which is, to some extent at least, *explicit*.

So, in thinking and talking about progression, we are asking whether there are better and worse ways of organising the time-sequence of experiences presented to children. Teachers have a great deal of intuitive 'knowledge' about progression, largely based in experience and tradition (including their own experience of being pupils, as well as their teacher training and socialisation as teachers). They have a 'feel' about what is appropriate at certain ages or stages, about what comes before what, about what should be delayed until later, and so on. Some of these ideas are based on views about children as learners, others on views of the subject matter. Apart from its intrinsic interest, research on progression is important because it may lead to other bases, more securely grounded in empirical data or theory, which can provide better guidelines for teachers (and others, such as textbook authors and curriculum planners) in making decisions about the actual sequence of events and experiences presented to the child.

Progression of Tasks or Progression of Learners?

Progression may be thought of in terms of the increasing demand of the tasks learners are given, or in terms of the increasing sophistication of responses to similar tasks. The former focuses on the nature of learning tasks. Syllabuses and programmes of study frequently embody such notions of increasing *task demand*. The latter focuses instead on the varying qualities of learners' responses to essentially similar tasks, seeing progression in terms of *task performance*. This sense of progression is particularly important in subjects, or domains, where tasks are relatively open-ended, permitting a wider range of possible responses. The distinction between progression in task demand and in task performance is used extensively by Qualter *et al.*, (1990) to structure their discussion of Sc1. These two senses of progression are, however, related through the single notion of progression in a learner's capabilities. This will be reflected in ability to perform the same (or similar) tasks in a more 'expert' manner, and ability to perform *more demanding* tasks. In the PACKS project we are interested to explore the nature of the understandings which lead to, or facilitate, progression in learners' capabilities in scientific investigating.

Models of Progression in Science

In science, it is useful to think about progression in understanding in distinct content domains, such as electric circuits, or forces and motion ('knowing what'); or progression in the ability to carry out specific tasks, such as setting up and using a microscope to look at cells ('knowing how').[1] In the former, the aim is greater 'understanding', in the latter we sometimes talk of greater 'skill'. There is, however, less difference between 'understanding' and 'performance' domains than is sometimes claimed (or implied). First, it is clear that many 'skill'-type performances depend upon having some knowledge and understanding. This is particularly so in the case of (so-called) 'skills' such as 'designing an experiment', but is also true in the example given above, setting up a microscope. Second, and perhaps more fundamentally, the only way we have of assessing a learner's 'understanding' is through some observable performance, such as their written or spoken answer to a diagnostic question, or their ability to engage appropriately in written or spoken dialogue about some phenomenon within the domain. That is, we have no direct access to 'understanding'; we infer it from specific features of observed performance just as we do in assessing the acquisition of so-called 'skills'. The task we have set ourselves in the PACKS project, of trying to understand the reasons for children's actions in carrying out investigations in science classrooms, is, therefore, more similar to the task facing someone who wishes to explore children's 'understandings' within a science content domain than might at first appear.

In any given science domain, whether the emphasis is on 'knowing what' or 'knowing how', we are interested in children's performance in relation to an idea of the 'ideal' performance which we want to help the child eventually to achieve. This comes from the structure of accepted knowledge in the domain, or the method followed routinely by members of the relevant scientific community in carrying out the practical operation in question. In some cases, these target performances may be simplified versions of the accepted scientific knowledge or practice. But they are derived from, and depend on the existence of, ways of thinking, talking and acting which are consensually agreed within the practising community of scientists.

In other words, ideas about progression in science have a strong *normative* dimension. They are about the movement of the learner from an initial 'novice' position towards (though not necessarily all the way to) a final position which is known in advance. However, knowledge about the desired end-point is not much help in curriculum planning; a more fully articulated model of progression in a domain will have to specify some of the intermediate stages between the novice position and the desired end point, and may also provide further guidance on the nature and causes of transitions from one stage to another.

It may be useful to classify models of progression in the following way:

Level 1: A model of progression at this level aims to specify a series of stages of understanding between a basic or 'novice' level and a more 'expert' one. These may be in a linear hierarchical sequence, or they may be organised as a more complex network. (The ten levels of the National Curriculum (DES, 1991) are an example of such a model. A more fully articulated version of this model is provided by NEAB (1992).) Traditionally such models were almost entirely analytic and *a priori*, based upon an 'expert' analysis of the logical structure of the domain in question. The differences between successive stages were seen in terms of rational principles, such as greater explanatory content or bringing a wider range of phenomena under a single explanatory framework, or as necessarily building upon ideas at previous stages.

The experience of the last twenty years of research into children's ideas in various science domains has shown us that models of domains based only on *a priori* reasoning may be seriously flawed. Empirical information from studies of the actual understandings of children about aspects of the domain (see, for instance, Driver *et al.*, 1994) may be necessary to test, refine and develop such models. The empirical approach cannot, however, replace the analytic one but can only supplement it; empirical studies depend on having some kind of analytic model to guide the enquiry. This becomes, essentially, a hypothesis which is tested against empirical data and rejected or modified in the light of the data. A developed level 1 model of progression in a domain is the product of an interaction between analytic and empirical approaches.

Such models may also have something to say, or will embody implicit messages, about the nature of the changes involved in moving between stages. A key distinction, noted by several writers, is whether the step involves knowledge 'accretion' or 'restructuring' (Rumelhart & Norman, 1981). West & Pines (1985) reflect the same distinction in their terms 'conceptual development' and 'conceptual change', while Carey (1985) talks of 'weak restructuring' and 'radical restructuring'.

Level 2: A model of progression at level 2 will seek to provide an account of the *reasons for changes* of understanding from one stage of a level 1 model to the next. An issue in constructing such a model is to decide what sorts of explanations for change will be allowed. At one extreme, a level 2 model may allow only rational, or epistemological, explanations for change. Changes might be accounted for as rational responses to new evidence which has been brought to the learner's attention. The well-known conceptual change model of Posner *et al.*, (1982) is essentially of this sort. In general, 'cognitive conflict' models of conceptual change tend to emphasise rational grounds for changes of understanding. Piaget uses the idea of 'equilibration' as the fundamental reason for development on rational grounds; it is 'the end of the line' for explaining why individuals seek to reduce conflict between existing schemata and new information. But level 2 models of progression might also use psychological variables such as: need-reduction, personality characteristics, social pressure, attention, motivation to achieve. Indeed a more recent revision of the Posner *et al.*, model (Strike & Posner, 1992) recognises the need to include a wider range of factors, including motives and goals, in describing a learner's 'conceptual ecology' and the ways in which it may change.

At both levels 1 and 2, a further distinction can usefully be made between models which aim to describe the progression of populations and those which are concerned with the progression of individual learners (see Table 4.1). All curriculum planning is based (usually implicitly) on at least a level 1 population model. In its details, it may contain some level 2 elements,

Table 4.1 A classification of models of progression

	Deals with populations	*Deals with individuals*
A 'map' of stages	Level 1 population	Level 1 individual
A 'map' of stages plus an account of reasons for moves from stage to stage	Level 2 population	Level 2 individual

but still in population terms. Teachers in their own classrooms may, of course, use strategies which draw upon their knowledge of individual learners. The classifications above also have some implications for research on progression. 'Snap-shot' studies of children's understanding in a domain can, at best, provide data for improving level 1 population models. Cross-age studies might be used to provide data for developing level 1 or level 2 population models. Short-term longitudinal studies (such as pre- and post-instruction designs) may provide useful data on specific transitions within level 2 models and can, in principle at least, provide data relevant to both population and individual models. Longitudinal studies of a cohort can also provide data on individual models at level 1 or level 2.

In terms of this classification, the PACKS project sets out to provide a level 1 population model of progression in the understanding required to carry out a scientific investigation. The PACKS data may also bear, albeit speculatively, on some aspects of a level 2 population model. Before considering how such models might be constructed, it may be useful to explore in a little more detail the nature of scientific investigations in the classroom and of the understanding involved in responding to such tasks.

Scientific Investigation

The focus of the PACKS project appears at first sight to be on a 'performance' domain rather than an 'understanding' domain (though it is important to bear in mind the point made earlier, that the similarities may be greater than often assumed). Carrying out an investigation is, however, clearly a complex performance, involving a series of distinct sub-elements which are linked together as a sequence of actions. This complexity distinguishes it from a more simple 'skill' such as using a microscope. It is also clear that decisions about how to proceed draw on understanding of the science domain in which the investigation is set, and on understanding of the procedures which should be followed in a scientific investigation.

It may be important, at this point, to clarify what is meant here by 'a scientific investigation'. The current interest in investigations in science is largely a consequence of the position they hold in the National Curriculum in Science, where Attainment Target 1 (Sc1) is about the ability to carry out scientific investigations. Essentially an investigation is an open-ended task. The NCC INSET Pack for Sc1 (NCC, 1991) begins by emphasising the difference between investigations and other sorts of practical work, in particular illuminative practicals, designed to illustrate an idea or theory, and to lead to a predictable conclusion which the learner can use to develop his or her understanding in a domain. By contrast, an investigation leaves the child to make decisions about what apparatus to set up, what to vary, what to measure, and so on. And the result is not a fact or relationship which the child is required to remember; the learning is about the procedures followed in collecting data to answer the original question posed.

Neither the National Curriculum nor its supporting documentation, however, says explicitly what it takes a 'scientific investigation' to be. Instead, some pointers are provided or implied by the statements of attainment (SoA) and various associated NCC publications. The SoA emphasise relationships between variables and use the number and type of variables involved as a criterion of increasing 'task demand'. The Non-Statutory Guidance (NCC, 1989) strongly reinforces this 'variables perspective' on investigations. Sc1 has been criticised by some for appearing to limit 'scientific investigations' to explorations of the relationship between a dependent variable and one or more independent variables.

In the PACKS project, we have taken an 'investigation' to mean a task (whether given or self-imposed) which involves the collection and use of empirical data (observations or measurements) to answer a question. This definition is very wide. It encompasses enquiries in the social sciences as well as the natural sciences, and might even be claimed to include historical enquiry. So a 'scientific investigation' must meet some additional criteria; but it is quite difficult to say precisely what these are. The boundary between science and other forms of enquiry is a matter of perennial scholarly debate (see, for example, Bernstein, 1983). Many of the issues involved need not concern us here, and to discuss them at length would be a diversion from the main theme of this chapter. Two specific points, however, may be worth stating explicitly. First we would include technology/ engineering tasks within the science domain because of the similarities of subject matter and of conventions about purposes and explanatory styles (causal, non-teleological, etc.). So 'scientific investigations' in our usage may be of artefacts as well as of natural phenomena and materials. Second, 'scientific investigations' include enquiries which are *not* about relationships between variables, although these remain an important sub-category. In fact the investigations we used in the PACKS project *are* of the variables type, as these do provide insights into the questions we are focusing on and are acceptable to teachers and pupils because of their obvious similarity to Sc1 type.

As the domain of interest of the project might be described as 'empirical enquiry in the scientific mode', it may be important to say a little more about the relationship between empirical enquiry and scientific enquiry. Another strand of criticism of Sc1, particularly in its first (DES, 1989) formulation, was that it took a rather naive empiricist view of science. Investigations cited as examples were set in atheoretical contexts, such as the waterproofness of cloths, or the absorbency of paper towels.[2] The Sc1 view appeared to give insufficient recognition to the fact that variables arise from a theoretical view of the phenomenon being investigated and that science is more than simply the collection and codification of empirical data. The revised version of Sc1 (DES, 1991), by insisting that assessment of Sc1 be carried out using investigations which include three distinct strands (predict/hypothesise, observe/measure, interpret/evaluate), can be seen as an attempt to address this issue. This revision has, however, raised further problems at the practical level; there appears, for example, to be a rather small number of phenomena which can be the subject of genuine, theory-based predictions (as opposed to guesses or hunches) at school level *and* which can be investigated empirically using school equipment.

It would require a much longer chapter to explore these issues in detail and to propose a set of criteria to characterise 'scientific investigations'. Since, however, all scientific enquiry involves empirical enquiry (although the converse does not follow, and involves difficult issues of demarcation), a certain level of competence in (and hence of understanding of) empirical investigation is a necessary, though not a sufficient, condition for carrying out a scientific investigation. Therefore, observing children's responses to empirical investigations may provide useful information about aspects of their understanding which are necessary for carrying out a scientific investigation. And empirical investigations may provide a teaching medium for developing understandings which are necessary for carrying out scientific investigations.

Performance of an Investigation Task in Science

In order to explore children's performance in scientific investigations in relation to their understanding, we developed seven investigations, involving topics in biology, chemistry and physics. Small groups of children, at ages 9, 11 and 14, were closely observed as they carried out each of these investigations within a normal classroom setting. Each group was asked to write down their prediction about the outcome of the investigation, and their reasons for this prediction, before beginning. A researcher kept field notes on the performance of the groups observed and also conducted impromptu interviews with the children to clarify their reasons for the actions they were seen to be undertaking. These were tape-recorded. A more formal interview was conducted with each group after completion of the task. The children were then also asked to respond to probes (administered orally to 9 year olds and in written form to 11 and 14 year olds) designed to elicit their ideas about science content and investigation procedures relevant to the investigation they had just completed. The children's own written record of their investigation was also collected. This entire set of data was then used to produce a detailed case record of each group's performance on the investigation task, which included verbatim extracts from interviews.

In order to approach the question of progression, it is necessary to try to describe the stages of, and the understandings implicitly required for, a response to an investigation task. This is not a trivial task. In recent years, the introduction of practical assessment in GCSE Science, the advocacy of 'process science', the work of the APU and the discussions surrounding National Curriculum Attainment Target Sc1 have produced a variety of terminology about the 'knowing how' aspects of science learning. There is little agreement about terminology and no evidence of an agreed underlying model of the domain. This contrasts with the situation in most 'knowing what' domains in science, where working models *are* available, based on a mixture of *a priori* and empirical inputs (as discussed earlier), the precise composition of the mixture varying from domain to domain. A comparable model of the 'knowing how' domain would be a major step forward and would provide a springboard for further work.

A simple model of the thinking involved in investigating is shown in Figure 4.1. This indicates that, in order to 'transform' the given task information into a sequence of actions (the 'task performance'), some 'processor' in the brain must select and access certain types of stored knowledge, and must integrate these into a plan of some sort which allows practical action to begin. Figure 4.1 proposes (in line with the terminology of APU, 1987: 50ff) that the accessed knowledge might be usefully divided into two categories, the relevant declarative (or conceptual) knowledge about the science domain of the investigation, and procedural knowledge about investigating in science. These two categories have been further sub-divided to indicate a possible hierarchy within each.

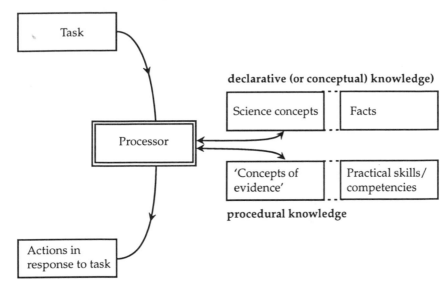

Figure 4.1 A simple model of the understanding which underpins investigation performance

This simple model does not, however, provide a basis for seeking to link specific aspects of understanding to specific stages in the performance of the investigation. For this, a model like that shown in Figure 4.2 is necessary. Before providing a commentary on this model, it may be useful to make clear that it is the product of an interplay between analytic and *a priori* reasoning on the one hand and empirical data from children's actual responses to investigation tasks on the other. It has been refined as the project has progressed, in the light of the data collected. So that data cannot be used as a 'severe test' of the model. It can, however, be used to validate the model by showing how it can accommodate and illuminate the varieties of performance and understanding observed. A future project could, however, set out to test the model.

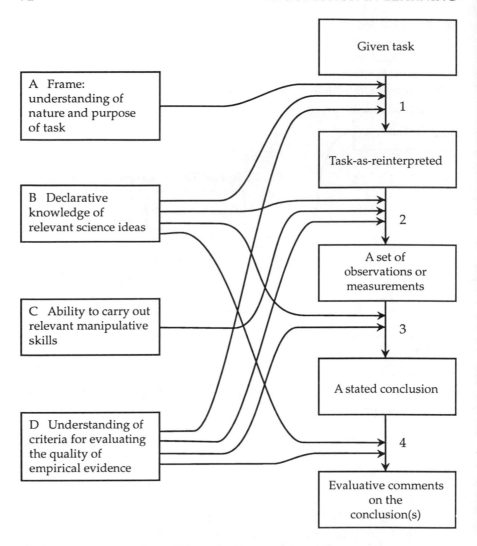

Figure 4.2 Carrying out a scientific investigation task: stages of performance and 'types' of understanding involved

The points which follow provide a commentary on the model of
Figure 4.2.

1. The five boxes which summarise the stages contain 'objects' – things
    which are produced (or may be produced) in the course of the
    investigation.

2.   The numbered vertical arrows identify actions. The grounds for these are not directly observable. We can only infer them, either from the 'objects' produced (in the sense above) or from the accounts children give to explain why they are doing what they are doing (or why they did what they did).

     If we use the term 'skill' we are referring to the quality of the actions represented by the numbered vertical arrows. This 'quality' may be reflected in the nature of the decisions taken or of the specific actions performed in moving from one stage to the next.

3.   The stages of an investigation are shown in Figure 4.2 as a linear sequence. In practice, children may go back from a later stage to revisit an earlier one, perhaps in the light of trials and experience, or as a result of a re-think (see APU, 1987: 24). Feedback loops of this sort have been omitted in Figure 4.2 for clarity only. The model should be read as including the possibility of such loops from any stage to any previous stage.

4.   The model leaves open issues of the structure of the contents of the 'knowledge boxes'. It is likely to be useful to think in terms of different types of memory element (see, for example, White, 1988: 22ff.) within each category. One important type is likely to be what White terms an 'episode' and others (Schank & Abelson, 1977) have called a 'script'. Adoption of a 'cooling curve' arrangement for our 'Cool Drink' investigation (which is described more fully in the next section of this chapter), and aspects of the use of the notion of a 'fair test', for example, might be seen as scripts for the two types of understanding.

5.   The distinctive feature of the model is that it identifies four different types of understandings which are brought to bear in taking decisions about actions. These are: understanding of the purpose of the task (frame), declarative understanding, skill in carrying out manipulations and understanding of evidence. The first, third and fourth of these together comprise *procedural knowledge*.

     Frame refers to the child's understanding of the nature and purpose of the task. Some children interpret a scientific task (involving the relationships between variables) as an engineering task (optimising the effect of variables) (Schauble, Klopfer & Raghavan, 1991). We have also observed two less sophisticated frames, which we term 'modelling' and 'engagement'.

     Declarative understanding refers to the child's understanding of facts, ideas and concepts in the science domain with which the investigation deals.

Understanding of evidence refers to the child's awareness and under-standing of criteria for assessing and evaluating the quality of empirical evidence. A key notion is the idea of reliability of data. In some investigations, understanding the idea of a variable, and perceiving phenomena in terms of relations between variables, is also a central aspect of understanding within this category. If more than one independent variable is involved, knowing how to ensure that a conclusion can be logically drawn from the set of data collected becomes important.

We are particularly interested in the ideas that children draw from each of these three sources to carry out each of the steps identified by the numbered arrows and how they use these ideas. The arrows linking the knowledge boxes to the stages of action show where understandings of each type may be brought to bear. So, for example, if we take a decision to repeat measurements to indicate an understanding of the notion of reliability, this might be evident at the planning stage (arrow 2), or the decision might be taken later in the light of events (as a loop back initiated during arrow 3). A decision about the choice of range of an independent variable, or about the value chosen for a control variable, is also an indication of an understanding of reliability, but is more likely to be built into the performance at the planning stage (arrow 2). The interpretation of small differences in measurements, which also depends on an under-standing of issues concerning the reliability of data, arises at the stage of drawing conclusions (arrow 3) or evaluating these conclusions (arrow 4).

Illustrating the Model in Action: Responses to the 'Cool Drink' task

We will now illustrate how the model of Figure 4.2 can be used to explore progression in children's ideas about the procedural dimension of science. The Cool Drink investigation task is set in the context of a cool bag used to keep a drink cool on a hot day. Children are asked to 'find out how the thickness of the padding affects how well a cool bag works'. For the task, groups of children are provided with a clock, a thermometer, and a range of containers such as beakers and measuring cylinders. They have access to a supply of ice-cold water, but the use of any type of tap water is not excluded. They also have access to a supply of three types of common wrapping materials: fleece, bubble wrap and foam. Each group is shown how they can vary the thickness of the wrapping by using different numbers of layers. After completing the investigation, groups were also asked to answer some diagnostic questions about key science ideas and aspects of scientific procedure relevant to this particular investigation. Responses to the task and the probes showed a range of understandings of the purpose of the task (frame), of thermal processes, and of the reliability of data. In view of the space available, the discussion below is necessarily selective and considers only some of the aspects of understanding explored by this task; a fuller account can be found in Lubben & Millar (1994).

Understanding the purpose of the task: Frame choice

In children's responses to the task, we noted examples of four distinct frames, or conceptualisations of the task, three of which could be further subdivided:

Engagement frame	1	Engagement and activity with the apparatus provided without obvious plan or purpose
Modelling frame	2A	Modelling to produce a desired physical appearance
	2B	Modelling to produce a desired effect
	2C	Modelling to produce a desired phenomenon
Engineering frame	3A	Random engineering: optimising the desired effect by trial and error
	3B	Iterative engineering: seeking a combination of factors which optimise the desired effect
Scientific frame	4A	Scientific empirical (comparison): using 2 values (often extreme values) of independent variable
	4B	Scientific empirical (trend): using 3+ values of independent variable to identify a trend
	4C	Scientific empirical (relationship): using 3+ values of independent variable to find a functional relationship
	4D	Scientific explanatory: using measurements to test a prediction based on an explanatory model, as a means of exploring the usefulness of that model

Frames 1 to 3A might be classed as novice frames. The higher levels of frame require planning and use of data for further investigation and so contain some more 'expert' aspects.

The Cool Drink task is open to interpretation in terms of a variety of frames. The given task asks children to explore the relationship between two variables: the thickness of the padding and the temperature change, and so is posed within a scientific frame. Many groups, however, re-formulated the task in an alternative frame.

For some, investigating appeared to be characterised by activity – the pressing need of the children seems to be to 'do something', believing that this will satisfy the demands of the task. In the Cool Drink task, the engagement frame was relatively rare, though it did appear in the determination of some groups to use of all the different types of containers provided. This was found more frequently with Year 4 children than with Year 7 or Year 9.

Several pieces of evidence were taken to indicate a modelling frame (2A). One was an explicit justification of the choice of the measuring cylinder as the container in terms of its similar shape, e.g. 'because it looks more like a cool bag' (stated by several Y7 and Y9 groups) and the comment that 'we should have tested it on a proper drink bottle or flask' (a Y9 group). Another was the indiscriminate wrapping of the container in padding material. Typical pupil comments associated with this response are: 'We have made a proper cool bag. It [the bubble wrap] is all over.' 'Cool bags are always like that. They are all covered. Everywhere. To keep the food fresh, and the drink fresh.' (Y9 group). Another Y9 group explained their choice of observation period: 'We tried it [measuring the temperature change] for 2 minutes and it stayed the same. So we'll try it for longer.' 'Yes, because if you have a cool drink, you are not going to put it in, and then drink it after 2 minutes, are you?'

In frame 2B, the aim is to produce the desired effect, in this case a decreasing or low temperature. One indicator of frame 2B is when groups work with only one set-up and want only to establish whether their set-up 'works' (examples from Y4, Y7 and Y9). Some groups show that they are working within this frame by treating readings which do not show a constant or decreasing temperature as indicating 'failure' or proof that 'the experiment doesn't work' (groups at Y4, Y7 and Y9), even to the extent that no conclusions are drawn and only readings are reported. Several methods were used to encourage the temperature to go down: add more water, or rearrange the 'cold' material (a Y4 and a Y9 group), test another 'cold' material (Y7 group), stuff the 'cold' material inside the beaker (Y4 group), soak the padding material around the container in ice-cold water (Y4 group), use new or additional (cold) water (Y4 and Y7 groups), use different types of water, including hot tap water which provides a satisfactory drop in temperature (Y4 group).

A random engineering frame (3A) was used frequently by groups of all three ages, as when groups decided to 'find out which type of material is the best one to keep the liquid cool', or when combinations of materials were compared for effectiveness (instances at Y4, Y7 and Y9). This is a complete re-formulation of the given task, focusing on type of material rather than thickness of material as the independent variable. A similar engineering frame may, however, be adopted with thickness as the independent variable: the task is conceptualised as finding the thickness which makes the temperature fall most (groups at Y4 and Y9) or fastest. One Y9 group used four beakers with increasing thickness of foam, intending to 'time how long it takes for each beaker to drop in temperature and then see which works best'. Some groups show that they are using a random engineering frame (3A) when asked to draw conclusions, which are formulated in terms of an optimum.

A scientific (comparison) frame (4A) is characterised by the use of two thicknesses and a conclusion drawn in the form of a comparison (or even a trend) (groups at Y4, Y7 and Y9). This example is taken from a Y9 group:

> For their first trial the boys measure consecutively the temperature at 1 minute intervals over 5 minutes for 2 beakers with 100 ml of cold tap water, one wrapped in one the other in two layers of fleece 'to see if two layers keeps it cooler'. The starting temperature is reported as 14 degrees for both beakers. The results (in table form) show an increase over 5 minutes from 14 to 16 degrees with one layer, and from 14 to 15 degrees with two layers. The boys conclude that 'the thicker the insulation the longer the water stays cool'. They generalise from a 2-point comparison.

If a scientific (trend) frame (4B) was adopted, groups used more than two data points (many examples at Y7 and Y9). This example is of a Y9 group:

> As the first trial the boys plan to use 10 ml of ice-cold water in a cylinder wrapped in one layer of foam, and measure the temperature every minute for 10 minutes. They include a reading at the beginning. They use the same procedure for a measuring cylinder without any padding, and with 2 and 3 layers of foam respectively.
>
> The final temperatures decrease with increasing numbers of layers of padding.
>
> They conclude that 'the more padding you put on, the cooler it stays' or 'the more insulation, the longer it takes to warm up'.

Drawing a graph of temperature change against thickness, or stating the conclusion in terms of a relationship ('as the thickness increases, the temperature rise in 10 minutes gets less'), were taken to indicate a scientific (relationship) frame (4C).

Some groups appeared to alter frame during an investigation, or to use a different frame in carrying out the task and in stating conclusions, but three-quarters of all groups used a stable frame (frame 2, 3 or 4) during the investigation. It is also interesting that over 75% of the changes of frame which occur are towards an engineering frame. This is an improvement if a group starts from a modelling frame, and we could claim that learning has taken place during the investigation. Several groups, however, also regressed from a scientific frame to an engineering frame.

Table 4.2 summarises the choices of frame for the Cool Drink investigation by children of the three different ages involved. Where a group used more than one frame during the task, the frame they used when formulating their conclusions has been taken to indicate their 'main' frame.

Table 4.2 Number of groups choosing each investigation frame (percentages in brackets)

'Main' frame	Year 4	Year 7	Year 9
Modelling frame	6 (37)	6 (19)	7 (22)
Engineering frame	6 (37)	17 (53)	13 (41)
Scientific frame	4 (25)	9 (28)	12 (37)
	16 (100)	32 (100)	32 (100)

This shows a clear shift between Y4 and Y7 away from the modelling frame and towards the engineering frame. Another change occurs between Y7 and Y9, from the engineering frame to the scientific frame. Even at Y9 level, however, fewer than half of the groups used a scientific frame for a scientific task, and the choice of an engineering frame was still very common.

Understanding of thermal processes

Research on children's ideas about heat and temperature (Erickson & Tiberghien, 1985; Driver et al., 1994) has indicated that some children of age 9–14 are likely to use a 'heat capacity' model of thermal phenomena based on the idea that some materials 'contain' (a lot of) heat, while others 'contain' coldness or less heat. Other children are likely to use a 'heat flow' model in which padding material is seen as a barrier to heat transfer from an object at a high temperature to one at a lower temperature. For convenience we will refer to the heat capacity view as model 1, and to the heat flow view as model 2. These differences in declarative understanding of thermal phenomena are likely to surface in groups' performance of the Cool Drink task.

Groups' understanding of thermal processes were probed using diagnostic items, given to the children after they had completed the investigation task. Table 4.3 shows the pattern of groups' responses to these probes. This indicates a shift with increasing age towards model 2 and away from the indecisiveness of using different models in different situations. The sample, however, is rather small at all age levels.

Table 4.3 Number of groups using each model of thermal processes in their probe responses

	Year 4	Year 7	Year 9	Total
Model 1: hot/cold materials	2	3	1	6
Mixed-model	13	20	16	49
Model 2: barrier	1	9	15	25
Total	16	32	32	80

It is interesting, however, to look at the relationship between the model of declarative understanding indicated by probe responses and the frame choice of the group in carrying out the task. This is shown in Table 4.4 (the entries in this table are the reference numbers of the pupil groups, the initial digit 1 indicating a Y4 group, 2 a Y7 group and 3 a Y9 group). This shows a clear association between declarative understanding and frame choice. Most of those groups who consistently use (the more scientific) model 2 in the probes adopt a stable scientific frame. Of the small number who consistently use model 1 in the probes, most use a modelling or engineering frame. In contrast, there is no clear pattern in the frame choice of those groups who used mixed models in the probes. Only 8 (of 49) adopted a stable scientific frame, but the group is fairly evenly divided between modelling and engineering frames, with 13 and 15 groups respectively adopting stable versions of these frames. Among these groups transition from one frame to another is also quite likely.

Table 4.4 Model of thermal processes used in the probes and frame choice in the task

Frame choice	Model of thermal processes (in probes)			
	Model 2 (barrier)	Model 0 (mixed models)	Model 1 (hot/cold materials)	Total (80)
Stable modelling frame **(type 2)**	203, 322	109, 110, 111, 113, 116, 204, 211, 223, 310, 313, 316, 327, 329	216	
	(2)	(13)	(1)	**16**
Transition: modelling to engineering frame **(type 2–3)**	207, 315	106, 206, 220, 309, 311, 330	105	
	(2)	(6)	(1)	**9**
Stable engineering frame **(type 3)**	303, 314, 317, 332	103, 114, 202, 205, 209, 212, 218, 221, 226, 230, 231, 320, 325, 326, 333	112, 208, 229	
	(4)	(15)	(3)	**22**
Transition: scientific to engineering frame **(type 4–3)**	232, 233	115, 228, 306		
	(2)	(3)	(0)	**5**
Stable scientific frame **(type 4)**	102, 217, 222, 224, 225, 227, 305, 307, 308, 319, 321, 328, 331	101, 107, 108, 201, 213, 215, 323, 324	318	
	(13)	(8)	(1)	**22**

Table 4.4 *(continued)*

Frame choice	Model 2 (barrier)	Model 0 (mixed models)	Model 1 (hot/cold materials)	Total (80)
	Model of thermal processes (in probes)			
Various other transitions between frames (type ?)	302, 304	104, 210, 219, 312		
	(2)	(4)	(0)	**6**
Total	**25**	**49**	**6**	**80**

Looking at the data from the perspective of frame choice, 80% of those groups using a stable modelling frame were mixed model users in the concept probes. Of those using the stable engineering frame, 65% were mixed model users in the probes, with the remaining 35% evenly divided between model 1 and model 2 thinkers. Of those groups using the stable scientific frame, only 40% were mixed model users in the probes, with almost all of the others using model 2. It would appear from these data that a clear, and more scientific, declarative understanding goes hand in hand with the use of a scientific investigative frame. Holding alternative or ambiguous concepts is associated with stable modelling or engineering frames, and often results in transition between frames.

It is also significant that the thirteen 'expert' groups with firm model 2 understanding and using a scientific frame throughout form a consistent behavioural cluster, as 11 of them also show consistent model 2 reasoning *in the task*. We note that the cluster consists mainly of groups at secondary level.

Understanding of reliability of data

The conclusions children draw at the end of an investigation may differ in the extent to which they are supported by the data collected. Sometimes the conclusion is well-supported by the data. On other occasions, a conclusion may be drawn which is not contradicted by the data, but where the data provides weak and unconvincing evidence for the conclusion. This may be so even where a scientific understanding of the situation investigated suggests that the conclusion offered is in fact correct. On yet other occasions, children may draw conclusions which are contradicted by the data.

Most groups interpreted the Cool drink task as a comparison of two (or more) materials or two (or more) thicknesses of material. Conclusions were therefore based on observed differences between data. When groups drew conclusions on the basis of differences in their measurements of only 1°C, they were classified as showing a 'weak' understanding of reliability issues in drawing conclusions. Where the conclusion was based on a reported difference of 2°C, this was classified as showing a 'partial' understanding of reliability issues in drawing conclusions. And where the conclusion was based on differences of more than 2°C, these conclusions were deemed to show a 'good' understanding of reliability issues in drawing conclusions, the assumption here being that the design of the investigation had (deliberately) ensured that the differences would be clear. Several groups provided additional and perhaps better access to their perceptions of the criteria which data must satisfy if they are to be used reliably for drawing conclusions.

A few groups measured the effect of the thickness by recording the time it took the water temperature to increase by a fixed number of degrees. In this strategy the thickness is the independent variable, temperature rise is the control variable and time is the dependent variable. This strategy has the distinct disadvantage that it is very difficult to judge exactly when the water has increased its temperature by 1°C. Those who persisted with this strategy were deemed to show little understanding of criteria for assessing the reliability of data. Their conclusions are classified as showing a 'weak' understanding of reliability issues in drawing conclusions.

Many groups, however, realised that the very gradual change of temperature was a problem and modified their strategy to one of measuring the temperature increase over a fixed time period for various thicknesses, i.e. with the thickness still as independent variable, the time as a control variable and the temperature rise as dependent variable. Such a change of strategy was seen as an indication that the group recognised that their previous method would not generate reliable data and were able to act to improve this. Such groups were classified as having, at least, a 'partial' understanding reliability. The following extract from the case record of a Y9 group illustrates this line of reasoning:

> The first trial was planned as wrapping a measuring cylinder with ice-cold water with one and two layers of fleece respectively, and measuring the time it takes the water to rise 5 degrees. Even during the planning stage there was a proviso that 'if it takes too long, we measure how many degrees it goes up in 5 or 10 minutes'.

The temperature rise, indeed, was considered too slow so the strategy for the second trial was changed. The temperature was measured over 10 minutes at 2 minute intervals.

Several groups concluded from identical or near identical results that 'there are no differences' (one Y4 group, three Y7 groups and five Y9 groups). These groups have clearly recognised the need for a significant margin of difference in reaching a firm conclusion. In view of the general hesitance to report inconclusive results, such conclusions are classified as showing 'good' understanding of reliability issues in drawing conclusions. The example in Figure 4.3 comes from the case record of a Y7 group.

Each group member fills in a table as follows.

Time in (mins)	Temp (C) fleece + foam	Temp (C) pop paper + foam
0	7	7
1	3	4
2	4	4
3	3	4
4	4	4
5	5	5
6	6	7
7	5	7
8	5	6
9	6	6
10	6	7

No conclusions are drawn from these results, as the group feels that they 'don't tell which one is better'.

Figure 4.3 A case record of a Year 7 group

Table 4.5 shows the results of classifying levels of understanding of reliability issues as indicated by the group's handling of small differences in drawing conclusions. This shows a shift between Y4 and Y7 away from the 'weak' category and towards the 'good' category ($\chi^2 = 6.96$, 2df; $p < 0.05$), but little further change between Y7 and Y9.

Table 4.5 Understanding of reliability issues in drawing conclusions from data with small differences

Level of understanding	Year 4	Year 7	Year 9	Total
'Weak'	9	12	10	31
'Partial'	6	8	11	25
'Good'	1	12	11	24
Total	16	32	32	80

What Can We Say about Progression?

The preceding section has illustrated how the model of Figure 4.2 can be used to explore separate aspects of progression in children's understanding of ideas which underpin their performance of scientific investigations. The analysis of the procedural knowledge domain, summarised in Figure 4.2, is a significant clarification of the nature of this hitherto rather amorphous aspect of science understanding.

A central problem in teaching students about scientific investigating and in assessing students' work on science investigation tasks has stemmed from lack of clarity about the nature of the understandings involved in producing the wide variety of performances observed. As a result, assessments of performance have tended to be one of the following:

1. Global evaluations of the overall quality of students' work in response to a task. The complexity of the performance required in response to an investigation task, however, means that global measures of performance (scores) risk being unduly impressionistic. They are, in any case, not particularly helpful since the same global 'score' can be arrived at in very different ways; the relative weighting of different elements is necessarily subjective; 'failures' at one stage may foreclose the possibility of certain decisions or options at later stages.

2. Fragmented and piecemeal evaluations of discrete elements of investigation 'skill'. These leave the sense that the whole is appreciably greater than the sum of the parts and that the essence of investigation performance is not 'captured' by assessments of separate elements.

3. Focused rather narrowly on one aspect of investigation performance. The National Curriculum's focus on variables handling might be seen

as an example of this, leading to a relative neglect of other important aspects and a consequent effective narrowing of the definition of an 'investigation' in practice.

The value of the model of Figure 4.2 is that it proposes a small number of distinct aspects of understanding which underpin performance. These provide a means of characterising procedural understanding in science at school level. We might use these categories to assess the performance of individual learners and to produce a profile of their understanding. The elements of such a profile would include:

- understanding of the purpose of scientific investigations (as indicated by decisions about frame)
- understanding of key ideas about evidence in science, particularly the idea of reliability, an understanding of phenomena in terms of relationships between variables, and an understanding of the necessary logical structure of a data *set* from which conclusions about the effect of one variable may be drawn.

In addition to these, the student's understanding of the science ideas and models which relate to an investigation will significantly influence their actions and interpretations; and their competence in specific manipulative skills may limit the choice and precision of observations and measurements.

Lastly, and rather more speculatively, we might then raise some questions about the nature of the learning involved in moving from 'novice' to more 'expert' understanding and hence performance. While it is clear that learners' decisions about frame may depend on the actual investigation task they are given, there appears to be a hierarchy of frames. Although some of these ideas about purpose of scientific investigation may be picked up tacitly, there may also be a case, as we have said above, for a more explicit discussion of these issues at regular intervals during a child's school science programme.

The understanding of evidence category deals with ideas which relate to almost all empirical enquiry. It is reasonable to suggest that this is a domain about which all children, however 'novice', know a great deal. Every person must, from infancy, have well developed skills for finding out information about the natural world, simply in order to make sense of experience. So we should expect children to have some well developed 'prior ideas' (prior, that is, to formal instruction) about many aspects of our 'understanding of evidence' box. For instance, the realisation that repeat measurements or observations may yield different results, especially with biological systems, could quite plausibly arise from everyday experience, though this is unlikely to be formulated explicitly as a general principle. It may even be that many of the fundamental aspects of understanding of evidence are available for use from an early stage, perhaps even from infancy, but that the ability to reflect upon them explicitly and the development of the language to talk about them comes later.

On the other hand, some ideas, such as the idea of a variable, and of seeking a relationship between a pair of variables (as opposed to a comparison between two cases or a trend in the influence of a factor on an outcome), are rather specialised ways of thinking, which are specific to the scientific view, and unlikely to arise simply through experience. An understanding of this aspect of what it means to do a scientific investigation is necessarily learned. Other ideas about variables, in particular an understanding of the need to control variables and alter one at a time in order to be able to associate changes with a specific factor are regarded, within the Piagetian framework, as developmental and as evidence of the achievement of formal reasoning. This interpretation is not, of course, universally accepted and younger children appear, in some cases, to be able to understand the need to hold all other factors constant in order to explore the effect of one factor which is varied, particularly in the case of a simple comparison (a 'fair test').

In essence, therefore, we are putting the case for a domain-specific, knowledge-based account of progression in understanding and managing the procedures of scientific enquiry. The domain is the understanding of empirical evidence in science. Some of the necessary knowledge may be available to the child, but its application limited by the extent of their ability to talk about, and hence to reflect upon, their understanding in order to see how to apply it to the case in hand. In this sense, progression may relate closely to increasing language competence. Also, some aspects, particularly those associated with variables and control of variables, may be developmental.

The last of these has been much more widely discussed in the research literature than the others. We would suggest that, while this may play some part in accounting for aspects of progression in investigation performance, other aspects of understanding of evidence merit greater attention. The overwhelming impression of many of the PACKS case records is that lack of understanding of these are the major obstacle to satisfactory investigation performance for most children.

Notes

1. The terms 'knowing what' and 'knowing how' come from Ryle (1949).
2. These are atheoretical in the sense that the child is expected to treat the investigation as a purely empirical enquiry. Theoretical explanations of differences observed, or theoretical considerations which might lead to selection of objects or variables to investigate are well beyond the level of understanding of the child.

References

APU (Assessment of Performance Unit) (1987) *Assessing Investigations at ages 13 and 15. Science Report for Teachers: 9.* London: DES.

Bernstein, R. J. (1983) *Beyond Objectivism and Relativism.* Oxford: Blackwell.

Carey, S. (1985) *Conceptual Change in Childhood.* Cambridge, MA: MIT Press.

DES (Department of Education and Science) (1989) *Science in the National Curriculum.* London: HMSO.

— (1991) *Science in the National Curriculum (1991).* London: HMSO.

Driver, R., Squires, A., Rushworth, P. and Wood-Robinson, V. (1994) *Making Sense of Secondary Science. Support Materials for Teachers.* London: Routledge.

Erickson, G. and Tiberghien, A. (1985) Heat and temperature. In R. Driver, E. Guesne and A. Tiberghien (eds) *Children's Ideas in Science* (pp. 52–84). Milton Keynes: Open University Press.

Lubben, F. and Millar, R. (1994) *Children's Responses to the Cool Drink Task and Probes. PACKS Research Paper 1.* York/Durham: Department of Educational Studies/School of Education.

Millar, R., Lubben, F., Gott, R. and Duggan, S. (1994) Investigating in the school science laboratory: Conceptual and procedural knowledge and their influence on performance. *Research Papers in Education* 9 (2), 207–49.

NEAB (Northern Examinations and Assessment Board) (1992) Science framework. common themes. Syllabus for the GCSE 1994 Examination. Manchester: NEAB.

NCC (National Curriculum Council) (1989) *Science. Non-Statutory Guidance.* York: NCC.

— (1991) *NCC INSET Resources. Science Explorations.* York: NCC.

Posner, G., Strike, K., Hewson, P. and Gertzog, W. (1982) Accommodation of a scientific conception: Toward a theory of conceptual change. *Science Education* 66 (2), 211–27.

Qualter, A., Strang, J., Swatton, P. and Taylor, P. (1990) *Exploration. A Way of Learning Science.* Oxford: Blackwell.

Rumelhart, D. E. and Norman, D. A. (1981) Analogical processes in learning. In J. R. Anderson (ed.) *Cognitive Skills and their Acquisition* (pp.335–59). Hillsdale, NJ: Lawrence Erlbaum.

Ryle, G. (1949) *The Concept of Mind.* Harmondsworth: Penguin.

Schank, R. and Abelson, R. (1977) *Scripts, Plans, Goals and Understanding. An Enquiry into Human Knowledge Structures.* Hillsdale, NJ: Lawrence Erlbaum.

Schauble, L., Klopfer, L. E. and Raghavan, K. (1991) Students' transition from an engineering model to a science model of experimentation. *Journal of Research in Science Teaching* 28 (9), 859–82.

Strike, K.A. and Posner, G.J. (1992) A revisionist theory of conceptual change. In
    R.A. Duschl and R.J. Hamilton (eds) *Philosophy of Science, Cognitive Psychology
    and Educational Theory and Practice* (pp.147–76). NY: State University of New
    York Press.
West, L. and Pines, A. (eds) (1985) *Cognitive Structure and Conceptual Change.*
    London: Academic Press.
White, R. (1988) *Learning Science.* Oxford: Blackwell.

5 Progression in Learning about 'The Nature of Science': Issues of Conceptualisation and Methodology

JOHN LEACH, ROSALIND DRIVER,
ROBIN MILLAR AND PHIL SCOTT

Introduction

In studies which address students' learning of science it is important to be clear about the nature of the subject matter to be learnt. For example, science educators have talked about young people needing to know about the technical contents of science (e.g. Thomas & Durant, 1987), the purposes of scientific knowledge (e.g. Giere, 1991), the extent to which particular theories are validated and accepted within scientific communities (Duschl, 1990), and the processes by which knowledge is validated within scientific communities (e.g. Miller, 1983).

The epistemology of scientific knowledge and the social processes involved in the generation and validation of this knowledge is a subject of debate, and there are major literatures addressing these issues in the history, philosophy and sociology of science. This is not the place for a review of these literatures and their implications for science education, though it is worth considering some issues relating to the nature and purposes of the scientific knowledge to be taught and learnt through the school science curriculum.

A common image of scientific knowledge and the scientific enterprise presented through the school science curriculum is a *naive inductivist* view:

the basis for scientific knowledge is impartial observation of the natural world, followed by induction from a large number of observations to a general rule. The following representation is taken from a publication aimed at science teachers at the secondary school level:

> Scientific literacy is an essential capability for an educated young person. Newspapers, television and magazines, for example, call on knowledge of the function of machines and electrical devices, the effects of chemicals and drugs, the nutritional value of foods, the ecology of different parts of the world and the ethics of transplant surgery and genetics. Part of this literacy is the ability to seek out explanations for things. Pupils need to use their skills to devise ways of testing their ideas and the ideas of others, such as advertising claims, and to evaluate possible solutions to problems. (NCC, 1993: 4)

The image of the scientific enterprise presented is of individuals seeking explanations through a process of empirical testing and evaluation. This empiricist, individualist view of scientific knowledge and the scientific enterprise has been heavily criticised in the philosophy of science on several grounds: (i) it is not possible to collect data in a value-free way: observations are always made in the context of theory (Popper, 1969); (ii) the logic involved in proving an inductive knowledge claim itself relies on induction (Hume, quoted in Chalmers, 1982); the scientific enterprise is social rather than individual (Kuhn, 1962).

Although there are a range of contemporary perspectives on the nature of scientific knowledge and the workings of scientific communities, these perspectives do appear to share some basic features. For example, scientific knowledge is viewed as conjectural: it does not emerge from data as a result of unbiased observation and logical thought, but rather is created by people to explain data. Scientific knowledge becomes public knowledge as a result of social processes within scientific communities, rather than individual processes. Caution must be exercised, however, in suggesting that there is one 'nature of science' – scientific knowledge and practice are located in different contexts, where different norms may operate (Parusnikova, 1992).

Kuhn (1962) has illustrated the social context of scientific activity by describing episodes in the history of science where scientists work within paradigms of contemporary thought and activity. Theory change does not take place on empirical grounds alone: particular social conditions are also necessary. Once scientific knowledge is consensually agreed among groups of scientists, it can be written down and used to make predictions that may not be empirically testable for a long period of time (e.g. Chalmers, 1982).

Recent debates in science studies relate to the status of the knowledge produced by scientific communities, and in particular whether that knowledge is warranted by social or empirical processes. Several studies in the history and sociology of science portray the knowledge which emerges as a result of scientific activity as solely the result of social processes (e.g. Latour & Woolgar, 1979). This relativist position argues that there is no basis for knowledge to be a true reflection of the world, and therefore the idea of scientific knowledge progressing towards 'truth' is problematic. Rationalist traditions in the philosophy of science do not accept this position, arguing that although scientific knowledge can never be a true reflection of the world, there are rational ways in which the products of scientific communities can be evaluated.

In arguing for a 'modest realist' ontology, Harré (1986) accepts that our theories about the 'real' world are different from the world: they are different in both epistemology and ontology. For example, a 'theoretical' pendulum consisting of a point mass bob attached to a zero mass chord swinging without friction is clearly different from the 'real' pendula that are being modelled.

One purpose of the scientific enterprise is to produce internally and logically consistent knowledge, generalisable across as wide a range of phenomena as possible. The knowledge produced is, however, produced in particular institutional settings with particular purposes in mind (e.g. Latour & Woolgar, 1979). The 'everyday knowledge' used by individuals in their social and physical interactions is not, however, intended to be internally and logically consistent, nor to be generalisable in the way that scientific knowledge is.

This presents a number of questions to science educators exploring people's learning of science: what representations of scientific knowledge do learners of science bring to their learning? How does this influence their learning of science concepts? How do their images of scientific knowledge and the scientific enterprise itself change as a result of studying science? This study was designed to investigate the nature of students' representations of science in the age range 9–16, and to identify any progression in these representations. In the next section, a rationale for our interest in young people's understanding of 'the nature of science' is presented. We go on to describe methodological considerations in eliciting students' representations, and illustrate this by presenting results from one diagnostic instrument. The final part of the paper considers the notion of 'progression' in more general terms, and how data from cross-sectional studies can be used in particular educational contexts.

Focus of the Study on Young People's Understanding of 'The Nature of Science'

In recent years it has been proposed that a curricular aim of science education should be to engender an understanding of the nature of the scientific enterprise among students, as well as a knowledge of the technical contents of science (e.g. AAAS, 1989). In addition, it has been suggested that an ability to think about the nature of theories and their relationship to evidence may help students in learning about particular scientific concepts (Driver & Oldham, 1985; Solomon, 1991).

We have already argued that the scientific enterprise is a social enterprise, and that scientific knowledge is conjectural, going beyond the data; the research questions for this study relate to the ways in which young people represent scientific knowledge and the scientific enterprise.

There are important distinctions to be made between representations of *the scientific enterprise*, representations of *scientific knowledge* and representations of *personal knowledge*. We are interested in students' representations of the scientific enterprise: what domains do they think scientists attempt to explain, and on what basis do they think that scientists make knowledge claims? One might speculate that students interpret scientific activity through a variety of common cultural representations of science in the media and in school science teaching; it is certainly unlikely that school-age students have any direct experience of the workings of the scientific community to draw upon. The nature of these representations among students, and the ways in which they change between the ages of 9 and 16, is the main focus of enquiry of this study.

Direct probing of students' representations of aspects of the scientific enterprise is problematic, in that school students have no real opportunity to participate in the scientific enterprise; in most cases contact with science is through school science lessons. At some time in most students' lives, however, they are likely to encounter information about particular scientific communities, whether this is through the media, through school science or through particular professional or personal circumstances in adult life (Layton et al., 1993). At this stage, representations of the knowledge produced by scientific communities may be constructed. We felt it reasonable to assume that a knowledge of how students represent scientific activity as encountered in school science contexts (i.e. their *personal knowledge*) would be insightful in hypothesising about the issues facing them in coming to representations of science as located in particular scientific communities. The second line of enquiry of the study thus relates to students' representations of scientific activity in familiar school science contexts.

The final line of enquiry relates to students' representations of the processes through which scientists come to make knowledge claims. There is no reason to assume that students in the 9–16 age range will have detailed knowledge of the workings of particular scientific communities: their knowledge is more likely to be based on fairly superficial treatment of the subject in the science curriculum, combined with common cultural representations of scientists. The point of interest is therefore the ways in which students come to represent the social processes of scientific communities, when introduced to descriptions of the workings of such communities.

In this paper, the phrase 'the nature of science' is thus used as a shorthand for these three lines of enquiry: (i) the domains and purposes of scientific activity; (ii) the nature of the basis on which scientific knowledge claims are made; and (iii) the nature of the personal and social processes through which scientists establish knowledge claims.

Previous Research on Students' Understanding of 'The Nature of Science'

A major study investigating the nature of young people's representations of the domains of interest of scientists in their work has been carried out by Aikenhead, Fleming & Ryan (1987). A written survey instrument was used with a large sample of Canadian high school graduates (aged 16–20), independently from any teaching programme. A main finding of the study is that students tend to characterise the purpose of science as being the manufacture of artefacts, usually for the enhanced well-being of humankind. When the generation of explanations is mentioned as a purpose for science, these are often seen as simple mechanistic explanations, rather than more general explanatory theories. It is also reported that the conjectural nature of scientific theories tends not to be appreciated by students. Rather, they tend to view theories as emerging from observed features with changes in scientists' theories over time coming about through improvements in instrumentation (e.g. more powerful telescopes). Carey et al., (1989), Songer & Linn (1991) and Larochelle & Désautels (1989) have reported similar views about the epistemology of scientific knowledge among students in the secondary years, in the context of theories encountered in their own learning of science.

Young people's representations of scientific knowledge, and in particular the relationship between theory and evidence in scientific enquiry, have been investigated by both psychologists and science educators. In a classic study to describe differences between how very young children and older children use theories as tools in solving problems, Karmiloff-Smith & Inhelder (1974) noted a tendency for older children to gather evidence systematically from a theory, and to evaluate the theory in the light of such evidence. They suggest that presenting children with counter-examples did not in itself produce change in students' ability to relate theory and evidence. A similar claim was also made by Rowell & Dawson (1983) in the context of a study on the use of counter-examples to promote conceptual change in the context of explanations of floating and sinking. In addition, Rowell & Dawson noted that young people's espoused views about how they tackle problems involving theory and evidence, and the actual procedures that are used, are different.

A number of studies address the question of whether differences between younger and older students' ability to relate theory and evidence can be accounted for in terms of the development of general reasoning skills, or an increased ability to deploy particular reasoning strategies in certain contexts. Kuhn, Amsel & O'Loughlin (1988) describe a number of experiments where children and adults evaluate 'theories' in terms of particular data items. The theories that the students were asked to evaluate in this study were set in everyday contexts and were independent of scientific subject matter. The authors note an increased tendency for older students to think about theories and the evidence that relates to them as separate entities, and they account for this in terms of the development of general reasoning skills.

This explanation is, however, questioned by Samarapungavan (1991). She presents evidence that children as young as six years old are able to differentiate theories on the grounds of logical and empirical consistency, generalisability, and parsimony; caution should therefore be exercised in concluding that younger and older children have different capabilities for logical thinking.

No work has been identified focusing on the ways in which young people represent the processes through which scientists come to make knowledge claims.

Elicitation of Students' Representations of 'The Nature of Science': Methodological Considerations

A number of different approaches to eliciting students' representations of 'the nature of science' have been identified. The first approach is to ask a direct question such as 'Why do you think that scientists do experiments?' (Solomon, Duveen & Scott, 1993), or 'What does it mean to study something scientifically?' (Durant, Evans & Thomas, 1989). The problem with this approach is in interpreting responses. Students could answer with any one of a variety of 'scientists' in mind, and these may not be made explicit to the researcher. Similarly, the word 'experiment' may be used with a variety of different meanings (Leach *et al.*, 1993a). Scientists do, of course, do 'experiments' for a number of different reasons.

Alternatively, an ethnographic approach could be used. Young people could be observed while engaged in various activities as part of their school science learning, and inferences could be made about the representations of the domains of science or scientific knowledge which guide their actions. The problem with this approach is that the representations of the domains of science or the nature of scientific knowledge which guide young people's actions in the context of their own learning of science may not be the same as their representations of the domains in which scientists work or the nature of knowledge generated by scientists. For example, young people engaged in investigative work in school may well be aware that the purpose of the activity is to 'discover' the answer that the teacher will reveal at the end of the lesson – there is no reason to assume that they think of scientists' work in a similar way.

A third, intermediate approach involves designing tasks to be completed by young people, and then asking them to elaborate upon their actions and responses to questions in the context of the activity. The advantage of this approach is that researchers can select appropriate contexts for their interests, rather than waiting for these to arise in the classroom. Similarly, the context in which young people's representations apply is clearer than if a decontextualised question is asked. For these reasons this third approach has been used in this study.

As has been stated, we are interested in students' representations of the domains of science and the nature of scientific knowledge in the context of the work of scientists. We realise, however, that for most students in the 9–16 age range it is more likely that they will answer in terms of their own experiences of science from school and other cultural sources, than in terms of the work of scientists. In designing tasks on which students could talk about their representations of the domains and nature of scientific knowledge, it was necessary to identify conceptually rich contexts with which students are familiar, similar to those encountered by students in their learning of science, rather than the more generalised correlational hypotheses used by Kuhn, Amsel & O'Loughlin (1988). A number of contexts were trialled with students in the 9–16 age range. During these trials, we noted that pairs of students used talk to understand conceptual features of the context, and were therefore much better at addressing more complex metacognitive questions about the domains and nature of scientific knowledge, than individuals. Interviews were therefore carried out with pairs throughout the study. (There are still, however, cases where students' abilities to address the metacognitive questions of the probes are constrained by their conceptual understanding of the context.)

In this way, diagnostic instruments (termed 'probes') were designed so that each aspect of interest could be addressed in more than one context. Seven probes were designed for administration as interviews with pairs of students at ages 9, 12 and 16.

A further probe, addressing the processes through which scientists produce knowledge, was administered to whole classes of 16 year olds working in groups of four. This probe was administered as a whole class activity in order that students could be introduced to the workings of particular scientific communities, prior to carrying out activities through which we could make inferences about their representations of the processes through which these communities made decisions. It was not possible to administer this probe at ages 9 and 12 due to the level of background knowledge required by students.

Appendix 1 contains a description of the tasks, together with information about sample size.

We will now describe the design and administration of one probe, the Scientific Questions probe, and give some preliminary results. Further details of the Scientific Questions probe can be found in Leach et al., (1993b).

The Scientific Questions Probe: Students' Representations of the Domains of Science

The Scientific Questions probe was designed to elicit information about students' representations of the domains of science. In order to examine this, we presented students with a range of questions which they were asked to judge as questions that scientists would be interested in finding out more about ('scientific questions') or questions that scientists would not be interested in finding out more about ('not scientific questions'). We imagined that students might draw upon a number of factors in deciding whether a particular question is a scientific question. Such factors might be: the type of phenomenon that is the subject of the question; whether the question is open to empirical investigation; whether the question has strong associations with school science; or the amount of background theoretical knowledge required to address the question. A set of questions was drawn up which spanned these dimensions (see Appendix 2). The questions are diverse in that answering some required empirical evaluation, whereas others are not amenable to empirical enquiry at all. Some questions assume a high level of background knowledge on the part of the person answering the question whereas others do not. The domains of the questions include natural phenomena, as well as social, ethical and economic issues. By presenting these questions to students and finding out whether they see them as 'scientific questions', inferences can be made about the ways in which young people of different ages construe and demarcate science as a domain of knowledge.

Young people were interviewed in pairs. They were presented with the questions written on individual cards. They were asked to consider the question on each card and to say whether they thought it was a scientific question, not a scientific question or whether they were not sure. They were told that scientific questions are questions that scientists might want to find out more about. They were then asked to explain the reasons for their classification. The interviewer asked students to choose any scientific questions that they thought might be particularly interesting to scientists, and to explain their reasons.

Analysis

Students' responses were coded at a number of levels. At the first level, a record was made as to whether each question was classified as a scientific question, not a scientific question or the students were not sure. In practice, a variety of justifications for these classifications were made by students, and the second level of coding aimed to group similar justifications. The third level of coding aimed to draw together features of responses across the different questions. What differences did students note between the questions? What features of the questions were used in classifying as scientific questions or not scientific questions? Were these features used consistently across the questions? The same coding scheme was used across each of the questions. The major part of the analysis focused on students' justifications for classifying particular questions as scientific questions, not scientific questions or not sure. The justifications offered by students tended to focus upon three features, but at varying levels of specificity:

- whether the question is open to investigation
- the domain of the phenomenon in question and
- the personal and institutional characteristics and interests of scientists.

Coding categories, derived from these features of responses, were not treated as mutually exclusive; responses which referred to both the testability and the conceptual domain of the question received two codes. The coding sets for each of these features are given in Appendix 3.

At the end of the interview students were asked what factors, in general, make a question a scientific question. Analysis was designed to determine whether criteria were used consistently, and whether this changed with age.

A number of different representations of the nature of empirical testing required to answer the question, the domain of the question, and the personal and institutional characteristics of scientists, were noted in the study. These will be illustrated by considering two of the questions, 'How was the Earth made?' and 'Which is the best programme on TV?'.

Results

(a) How was the Earth made?

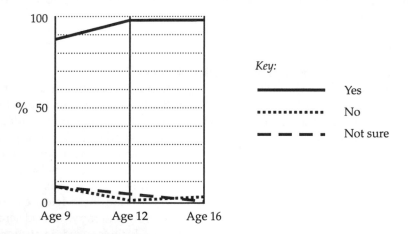

Figure 5.1 'Earth': Scientific question?

This question was almost unanimously classified as a scientific question at all ages – see Figure 5.1. The percentages of responses referring to empirical testing and the domain of the phenomenon are shown in Figure 5.2.

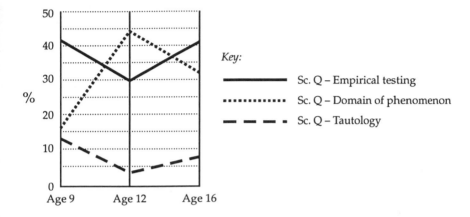

Figure 5.2 Earth: percentage of responses

At all ages, there was a tendency to offer a tautologous justification for classifying this as a scientific question. Subjects seemed so convinced that this is a scientific question that justification seemed irrelevant:

Interviewer: How was the earth made? Why are they interested in that?

Pupil: They want to find out how it was made and what it's made out of.

(Age 16)

There are interesting age-related trends in the ways in which subjects referred to both empirical testing and the domain of the phenomenon.

(i) Justifications relating to empirical testing. At each age, a number of responses referred to an unproblematic process of finding out how the world really was made (coded 'test if it happens'):

I: How was the earth made?

P: Well no one's sure really are they, so people are always trying to find out.

(Age 16; test if it happens)

At ages 9 and 12, a small number of responses suggested that scientists would be interested in this question because there is a process of making something involved (coded 'make a phenomenon happen'):

I: What made you decide that scientists would be interested in finding an answer to that question?

P: Well, they're trying to build a planet on Mars, because people think there was life on Mars years ago, and they might want to try and make it the planet that can live again, 'cause I've watched this programme and they want to see if they can put life on it again with special ways.

(Age 9; make a phenomenon happen, or stop it)

By ages 12 and 16 a number of more sophisticated responses about the nature of empirical testing were noted. A number of responses suggested that scientists would be interested in comparing mechanisms for how the Earth was made, to evaluate a theory (coded 'evaluate a theory'). Similarly, some subjects suggested that although the question is unanswerable, information from various sources could be used to compare theories (coded 'find a cause'):

P1: Yeah, well there's loads of theories to that. I mean, so called the 'big bang' and it could have just been one planet exploding, right. The core being sunk, 'cause that's meant to be the hottest part and then like just bits got in orbit round it and that slowly formed into planets.

I: And what makes that something that scientists . . . ?

P1: Well, yeah, because nobody actually knows how the earth was made. And everybody tries to think out why the dinosaurs with us. I mean, they all say that some big meteor hit the earth and span it round the wrong way and that's what killed everything.

I: Okay. Do you want to add anything to that?

P2: Yeah. They're still looking for evidence in everything. You know, like digging up things. Fossils and everything. Looking for special marks. It's got something to do with science.

(Age 16; evaluate a theory)

I: But what makes it a scientific point of view?

P: When you look into the crust and all the different parts of what it's made up and Bronze Age, and Iron Age and all that and all the chemicals and minerals and what made the Earth and everything.

I: Okay. What it's made out of and history.

P2: That sort of thing. Yeah, I should think would be scientific.

(Age 16; find the cause)

In general, there was hardly any reference to the difficulties of collecting empirical evidence for a process that has already happened.

The percentages of responses at each age using these forms of reasoning are shown in Figure 5.3.

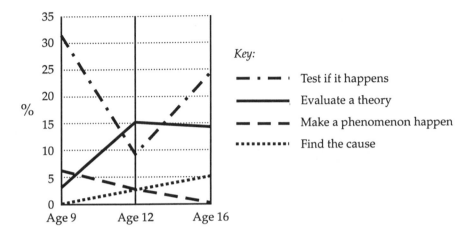

Figure 5.3 Earth empirical testing: breakdown of categories

There is an increase in the representations of empirical testing as being theory-based (i.e. 'evaluate a theory' and 'find the cause') with age.

(ii) Justifications relating to the domain of the phenomenon. In referring to the domain of the phenomenon, subjects referred to improving the quality of life by stopping polluting the Earth (coded 'quality of life'), a general interest among people in the history of their planet (coded 'social interest'), and the fact that the domain of the phenomenon is about the Earth (coded 'nature of the phenomenon'):

I: And why are scientists interested in something like the Earth do you think?

P: Because of pollution destroying it.

     (Age 9; quality of life)

I: Why would they be interested in that question?

P: Because they would want to know how it was made and that and people would want to know.

     (Age 9; social interest)

P: I don't know really. I just think it'd be interesting how you'd how you know your own planet had been made.

(Age 9; nature of the phenomenon)

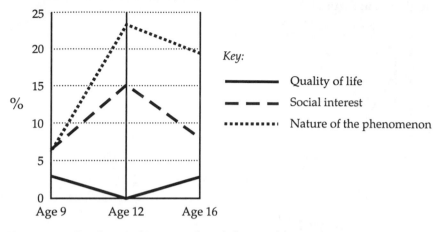

Figure 5.4   Earth social interest: breakdown of categories

The apparent decline between ages 12 and 16 in references to social interest and the nature of the phenomenon, are due to an increased number of responses referring to empirical testing.

(b)   Which is the best programme on TV?

The majority of subjects at each age suggested that this question would not be of interest to scientists, as can be seen in Figure 5.5.

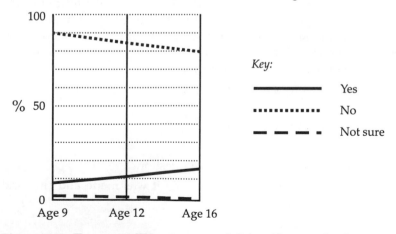

Figure 5.5   'Favourite TV programme': Scientific question?

There is a trend with age for more subjects to classify the question as a scientific question on the grounds that some empirical testing may be involved ($p < 0.084$). Of the subjects who stated that the question is not a scientific question, the most prevalent reasons were because the subject of TV programmes is outside the domains of science or that the personal characteristics of scientists preclude an interest in TV programmes. The percentage of responses at each age referring to each of these features is shown in Figure 5.6.

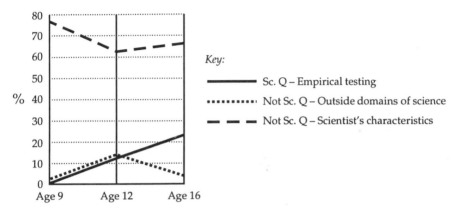

Figure 5.6 TV programme: percentage of responses

(i) Justifications relating to empirical testing. There are interesting trends in the ways in which subjects at different ages referred to empirical testing. Typically, at age 9 empirical testing was not mentioned. At ages 12 and 16 many responses suggested that it is possible to test empirically which TV programmes are the most popular (coded 'test if it happens').

A small number of responses at ages 12 and 16 suggested a rather more sophisticated notion of empirical testing, involving the need to operationalise some of the terms in the question such as 'best' (coded 'evaluate a theory'). Once these terms have been defined, then scientists can investigate which is the 'best' programme on TV:

P1: The best programme on TV, just about everybody has got a different favourite programme, so . . .

P2: But they do it and find out the most popular, yeah but, they don't find out the 'best'.

I: Oh I see. How would they find out the most popular?

P1: It would just be averages. They ask about 100 people and work out a percentage.

(Age 12)

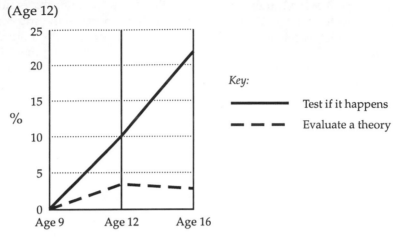

Figure 5.7 TV Programme empirical testing: Breakdown of categories

Figure 5.7 illustrates the percentage of such responses at each age: the increase with age in the number of subjects suggesting that the question is empirically testable is significant ($p < 0.062$).

(ii) Justifications relating to personal and individual characteristics. As well as mentioning empirical testing, a number of responses referred to the personal and institutional characteristics of scientists in classifying this question as a scientific question or not. A number of subjects suggested that scientists have no particular expertise to bring to bear on this matter (coded 'no special expertise'). Others suggested that the best TV programme is simply a matter of opinion (coded 'matter of opinion'):

P: It's like a question you get in a magazine. It's a matter of interest really. It's nothing really important.

(Age 16; no particular expertise)

P: Well that's to do with people's opinions it's not and you can't really say what's best and what . . . it just depends on your opinion.

(Age 16; a matter of opinion)

It is interesting to note that many such responses suggested that scientists are not interested in things that are a matter of opinion and therefore likely to change, but rather in phenomena that are predictable and lawful.

A number of responses referred to the personal characteristics of individual scientists. At age 9, many subjects seemed to draw upon a stereotyped image of scientists as people who would not watch the TV (coded 'stereotyped scientist'). No distinction was made between the personal interests of scientists and their professional activity, and it was concluded that scientists would not be interested in this question. Following similar lines, a number of responses suggested that scientists may have a personal interest in TV programmes, and may therefore investigate this question (coded 'personal motivation'):

I: Okay. So what is it about that that you think scientists wouldn't be interested in.

P1: Because they don't watch telly much and there would just be some boring programmes and things like that, and they wouldn't really be interested in programmes and TV.

      (Age 9; stereotyped scientist)

I: What was it about this one that made you decide that it was a scientific question? A question that scientists would want to find out more about?

P1: 'Cos there's quite a lot of good films on. (. . .)

P2: And good programmes.

      (Age 9; personal motivation)

A number of older subjects suggested that even though this question is open to empirical investigation, the investigators would not be scientists (coded 'narrow background'); companies would employ other people to do this sort of work:

I: Yeah. Which is the best programme on TV?

P: Oh that's a matter of opinion and it's [pause] erm sort of it'd have to be carried out by market research. Erm it's not really scientific at all.

      (Age 16; narrow background)

Figure 5.8 shows the percentages of such responses at each age. There is a change with age in the way in which subjects draw upon the personal characteristics of scientists. At age 9, a stereotyped view of the scientist as someone uninterested in 'worldly' matters such as TV programmes seems to prevail. At age 12 this view was not noted, though a number of responses seemed to suggest that scientists' work is governed by their everyday interest in matters such as TV programmes. By age 16, there was little mention of the personal characteristics of scientists.

There is a significant increase in the number of subjects referring to different professional groups carrying out market research work on favourite TV programmes ($p < 0.062$).

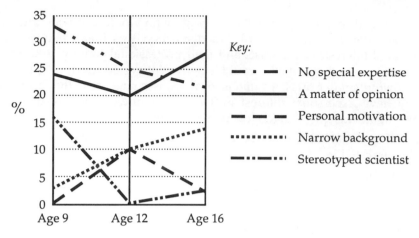

Figure 5.8 TV Programme personal/institutional characteristics: Breakdown of categories

Age-related changes in representations of the domains of science

As has been described, the questions presented to students differed significantly in context and amenability to empirical investigation. Not surprisingly, students justified their classifications of these questions according to different criteria; age-related changes in types of justifications do not necessarily occur across the full range of questions. None the less, it is possible to identify some changes that seem to occur in students' representations across a number of the questions.

In general, older subjects tended to offer more detailed justifications which drew upon a wider range of factors, than younger subjects. We did not note a tendency among subjects of any age to use criteria consistently across contexts: the tendency was to address each question as a separate case. At the end of the process of justifying each question as a scientific question or not a scientific question, subjects were asked what, in general, makes questions scientific questions. Their answers tended to refer to specific features of the individual questions, rather than making a more general analysis.

Responses referring to empirical investigation

In general, older subjects were more likely to refer to empirical testability as a criterion for scientific questions, than younger pupils ($p < 0.0008$), as shown in Figure 5.9.

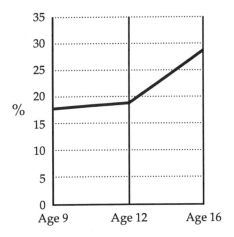

Figure 5.9 Empirical testing mentioned?

In all cases, but particularly the cases of the Earth and Atmosphere questions, there are clear differences in the ways in which younger and older subjects referred to empirical testing. Typically, younger students referred to an unproblematic process of finding out whether something really does happen, with little consideration of how this could be done in practice. By contrast, older subjects sometimes referred to a view that particular questions cannot be operationalised for empirical investigation, and are not, therefore, scientific questions. When older subjects did refer to empirical investigation, this was often more sophisticated in nature and suggested a need for knowledge of mechanisms rather than simply finding out whether something happens. For example, some older subjects suggested that in order to stop global warming it is necessary to know the cause of global warming as well as whether it is happening. In a small number of cases, subjects referred explicitly to an empirical process of data collection in order to evaluate a theory (such as a particular theory about how the Earth was made).

Responses referring to the domain of the question

A wide range of different responses mentioned the domain of the question. There was a strong tendency to classify questions seen as having particular significance to human beings (such as Atmosphere and Babies) as scientific questions. Many older subjects drew upon their knowledge of subjects in the school curriculum to classify questions as scientific, though in some cases the responses of older students suggested a more sophisticated view that scientists are interested in predictable natural phenomena rather than matters of public opinion. In the case of the Dolphins question, two responses stated that the question was ethical rather than scientific.

When discussing two possible explanations for the 'mystery' of whether talking to plants makes them grow better, older subjects tended to refer to whether they could see a possible mechanism in deciding whether scientists would be interested in the explanation. For example, the process of photosynthesis was often mentioned as a reason why scientists might investigate whether something from the breath affects plant growth. Between the ages of 9 and 12, significantly more responses refer to the domain of the question in justifying classifications ($p < 0.0028$).

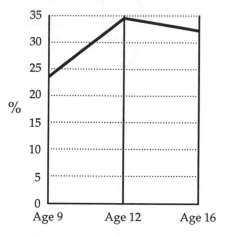

Figure 5.10 Domain of the question mentioned

Responses relating to views of the personal and institutional characteristics and interests of scientists

Again, a wide range of responses referred to the personal and institutional characteristics and interests of scientists. Although there is no age-related trend in the frequency of mention of the personal and institutional characteristics and interests of scientists, the representations of scientists used by younger and older students do differ. Typically, younger pupils did not differentiate the personal and professional interests of scientists, suggesting that as scientists are male and serious they would not be interested in babies' diet or TV programmes. In many cases older subjects showed a more sophisticated knowledge of the types of professionals employed to do various tasks, stating that market researchers, rather than scientists, would carry out particular forms of empirical testing.

Other responses

At age 9, a significant number of responses did not justify their classification in any way, other than by answering the question. Similarly, a number of younger subjects used tautologous reasoning, stating that certain questions are scientific 'because scientists would be interested in it'. This tendency seems to decline between age 9 and 12 ($p < 0.016$ across the six reported contexts), though this could be explained by the possibility that 9 year olds were less likely to understand our questions than 12 year olds, and therefore fell back upon tautologous reasoning.

The Notion of 'Progression in Learning Science'

In investigating progression in children's learning of science we have identified a number of different approaches to studying the general question of progression, each addressing different facets of the problem.

A commonly adopted strategy (and one used in the classical studies by Piaget and his collaborators) is that of mapping trends in the responses of children of different ages to the same task within the domain of interest. Such cross-age studies have enabled characterisations of students' reasoning in particular science domains to be identified and gross changes with age to be described. Research carried out into children's conceptions about the physical properties of air is an example of such a study (Brook & Driver, 1989). In this case it was noted that students aged 5–7 did not view air as substantive but by age 8 most students acknowledged the existence of air as taking up space. Between ages 8 and 12, however, they tend to consider air as having negative weight or to be weightless. The conception of air as occupying space and having mass and weight evolves during the secondary school years (maybe as a result of teaching). Such a study enables different representations to be identified and gives patterns of prevalence in children's reasoning at different ages. We see such studies as being useful in planning curriculum activities and materials appropriate to different age groups of children, as well as informing teaching interventions at particular ages. We view the present study as being of this type.

Such cross-age studies do not, however, address the issue of individual trajectories in learning. A longitudinal design is necessary for this. By following the same students over time a series of 'snap-shots' can be obtained to characterise individual learning trajectories. Questions such as the extent to which learners follow similar or different trajectories or the influence of particular instructional materials on learning trajectories can then be investigated. Such studies can also provide an empirical reference point for theorising about how conceptual change is characterised: is it a process of theory change as suggested by some scholars (e.g. Vosniadou & McClosky, 1992; Brewer, 1983) or does it involve piecemeal and parallel developments (e.g. Solomon, 1983)?

Such longitudinal studies can yield greater 'fine structure' in the routes individuals take in their learning. However, they still only provide a description of the route taken in learning. They do not provide information about the dynamics of the processes which 'drive' progression. For this, appeals need to be made to theories of learning. The current interest in theories of learning as conceptual change is one such approach to studying this problem.

Learning Science – What Progresses?

Different perspectives on learning science place differing emphasis on changes in various features as learning takes place, including individual cognitive changes (Carey, 1985; Kuhn, Amsel & O'Loughlin, 1988; Chi, 1992; Vosniadou & Brewer, 1992), socially mediated changes (Bruner, 1985) and attitudinal changes (Pintrich, Marx & Boyle, 1993). We view learning science as a process of enculturation where learners are encultured into scientific ways of knowing through social processes, making personal sense of scientific representations of phenomena in terms of their existing 'everyday knowledge' (Driver et al., 1994a).

Everyday ways of representing natural phenomena differ from scientific representations in terms of both their epistemology (the purposes and status of explanations) and ontology (the entities from which explanations are constructed). For example, many everyday representations are grounded in very narrow contexts: when describing a fire burning down 'to nothing' the aim is to produce an explanation specific to the context of burning fires, possibly with the pragmatic purpose of describing how much fuel is used and how much solid waste is left. The epistemological commitment of such everyday representations is to successful explanations in particular contexts. By contrast, a scientific explanation of the process of burning is grounded in a theory of chemical change: the main epistemological commitment is to produce generalisable, reliable explanations. Similarly, the ontology of everyday and scientific representations of burning differ in that everyday representations do not take account of gaseous products: the fire has burnt 'to nothing'.

A large research literature now exists on children's representations of natural phenomena and how these change with age (see Carmichael et al., 1990). From these studies, it is possible to make inferences about the nature of children's 'everyday ontologies'. For example, when a log fire burns down to a pile of ash, children state that matter is 'burnt away' (Andersson, 1991). Although older children may acknowledge that there are gaseous products, these are not viewed as 'substantive matter' having properties such as mass (Meheut, Saltiel & Tiberghien, 1985). Similar findings about children's representations of gases have been found in other physical and biological contexts (Stavy, 1988; Brook & Driver, 1989; Leach et al., in press a).

By contrast, there have been fewer studies of the epistemology of children's everyday knowledge and how this changes with age. This study is being undertaken to contribute to this field.

To be successful in learning science, children may have to construct new ontological entities (such as 'matter') as well as learning about the epistemology of scientific knowledge and how this differs from the epistemology of everyday knowledge. It is likely that progression in conceptual understanding of science involves an interaction between these features (Leach et al., in press b).

Uses of Data from Cross-sectional Studies

It is intended that this study, along with studies of conceptual trajectories of learners in particular conceptual domains, will help to provide a 'map' of progression in science learning across the school years. In turn, this can be used to inform intervention studies designed to promote learning, and curriculum design and sequencing (Driver, et al., 1994b).

It appears that progression in conceptual understanding of science involves complex, interacting changes in:

- the ways in which learners come to represent features of 'the nature of science' such as the nature of scientific knowledge and the domains of science
- the representations of particular phenomena available to learners
- learners' background knowledge about the characteristics of scientists and the institutional norms of the scientific enterprise.

Other features, such as changes in motivation to learn science, are also likely to be important.

It is not possible to describe individual trajectories in learning from cross-sectional studies. Cross-sectional studies do not give information about what children at particular ages *can* do, but rather what they *do* do in a given situation. For example, it is not valid to conclude that just because certain nine-year-old students did not refer to empirical testability, or conceptualised the nature of the empirical testing required for a particular scientific question in a non-standard way, they were not *capable* of such references or conceptualisations. On the one hand, it is possible that nine-year-old students are not able to think about theories as separate from the evidence that they attempt to explain, but on the other hand it could be that nine-year-olds are not clear as to what mode of response is appropriate in the particular social setting of the interview or the science classroom. Such questions about the underlying basis for progression cannot be answered through cross-sectional studies.

Data from studies such as this one can, however, be used to inform teaching interventions by highlighting possible mismatches between student representations of 'the nature of science' and the views underpinning the curriculum. For example, in the UK many science teachers use 'practical work' of various kinds as illustration for (or even 'proof' of) particular conceptual representations, with lower secondary school students. This research suggests that a number of such students may well think that the purpose of such work is to find out whether particular phenomena really do happen rather than to explain them. It may therefore be prudent for teachers to spend more time in making explicit the purposes of such activities.

Similarly, information about prevalent student representations of 'the nature of science' at different ages can be used to inform the sequence in which particular aspects of 'the nature of science' are introduced into the curriculum (Driver *et al.*, 1994b).

Acknowledgements

Liz Demsetz carried out many of the interviews for the study, and much of the coding. Her contribution to the quality of the data, her insights into finding meaningful ways to represent the data through analysis, and her ability to work to a demanding schedule are gratefully acknowledged. We also acknowledge helpful and challenging discussions with Dr Nancy Brickhouse about the design of the study.

Appendix 1. Probes used and sample size

Task name, and aspect	Focus of task	Description of task
Experiment *Nature of scientific knowledge*	Inferences are made about pupil's understanding of the the word 'experiment' and their ideas about the relationship between theory and evidence in experiments.	Pupils classify descriptions of people engaged in various activities as 'experiment', 'not experiment' or 'not sure', giving reasons. 30 pairs at ages 9, 12 and 16
Belief *Nature of scientific knowledge*	Inferences are made about the warrants seen as necessary for belief by pupils, and the status of theories.	Pupils are asked for their warrants for belief for specified commonly accepted theories about the shape of the Earth and the flow of electric current. 30 pairs at ages 9, 12 and 16
Theory stories *Nature of scientific knowledge*	Inferences are made about children's ideas about the status of theory and their relationship with empirical evidence.	Pupils respond to three stories in which theories are described, and asked whether characters in the story know about the basis on which the theories are true. 30 pairs at ages 9, 12 and 16
Real and imaginary *Nature of scientific knowledge*	Inferences are made about pupils' ideas about the status of theories, and their warrants for belief in theories.	Pupils respond to three cartoons in which contrasting opinions about the status of theories are raised. 30 pairs at ages 9, 12 and 16
Scientific questions *Purposes of science*	Inferences are made about the role of empirical testing, and the boundaries of the domains of scientific theories.	Pupils classify various questions on the basis of whether scientists might investigate the question or not. 30 pairs at ages 9, 12 and 16

Appendix 1 *(continued)*

Theory and evidence *Nature of scientific knowledge*	Inferences are made about the ability of pupils to differentiate theory from evidence, and the relationship between theory.	Pupils examine phenomena in the contexts of electricity and floating and sinking, and select theories to explain the phenomena. Empirical evidence is then presented for explanation using the theory. 30 pairs at ages 9, 12 and 16.
Plunger *Nature of scientific knowledge; purposes of science*	Inferences are made about the ways in which pupils conceptualise the processes involved in a school science activity.	Pupils watch a video of investigation performed by 13-year-old pupils in which they have to explain the phenomenon of a sink plunger 'sticking' to a surface. Pupils have to identify what they think the pupils are doing at each stage of the investigation, and why. 5 pairs at ages 9, 12 and 16
Closure of debates *Science as a social enterprise*	Inferences are made about the processes seen by pupils to influence the closure of a debate within the scientific community, and a debate on a scientific issue with broad social significance.	Pupils follow some teaching about the closure of debates within the scientific community, in the context of theories about Plate Tectonics and food irradiation. Pupils' views about the closure of debate are elicited prior to the teaching, during discussion and after teaching. Four classes of 16-year-olds.

Appendix 2. Questions used in the Scientific Questions probe

Question	Reason for inclusion
Which kind of fabric is waterproof?	Can be tested empirically, little theoretical background needed
Which is the best programme on TV?	Related to aesthetics
Is it wrong to keep dolphins in captivity?	Related to ethics
How do birds find their way over long distances?	High theoretical background required to inform work
What diet is best to keep babies healthy?	Can be tested empirically; high level of theoretical background
Is it cheaper to buy a large or a small packet of washing powder?	Related to economics
How was the Earth made?	High level of theoretical background
Is the Earth's atmosphere heating up?	Can be tested empirically; high level of theoretical background
Do ghosts haunt old houses at night?	Can be investigated empirically, but an unlikely conceptual area
What kind of bacteria are in the water supply?	Empirical testing; high level of theoretical background
Can any metal be made into a magnet	Empirical testing, little theoretical background. School science context

Appendix 3.   Coding sets used

Empirical

a1   Does it happen?

a2   Evaluate a theory

a3   Make a phenomenon happen, or stop it

a4   Find the cause

a5   Make measurements

a6   Make predictions

Tautology

b1   Tautology

b2   Answers the question

Domain

c1   Quality of life

c2   Social interest

c3   Natural phenomena

c4   Finding out anything new

c5   School science context

c6   Historical

Personal and institutional characteristics

d1   Substantive

d2   Research programme

d3   Stereotyped scientist

d4   Personal motivation of scientists

d5   Narrow background of scientists

Not sure/other

e   Not sure/other

References

AAAS (1989) *Science for all Americans: Project 2061*. New York: Oxford University Press.

Aikenhead, G. S., Fleming, R. W. and Ryan, A. G. (1987) High school graduates' beliefs about science-technology-society. 1: Methods and issues on monitoring student views. *Science Education* 71 (2), 145–61.

Andersson, B. (1991) Pupils' conceptions of matter and its transformations (age 12–16). *Studies in Science Education* 18, 53–85.

Brook, A. and Driver, R. in collaboration with Hind, D. (1989) *Progression in Science: The Development of Pupils' Understanding of Physical Characteristics of Air Across the Age Range 5–16 Years*. University of Leeds: Centre for Studies in Science and Mathematics Education.

Bruner, J. (1985) Vygotsky: A historical and conceptual perspective. In J. Wertsh (ed.) *Culture, communication and Cognition: Vygotskian Perspectives* (pp. 21–34). Cambridge: Cambridge University Press.

Carey, S. (1985) *Conceptual Change in Childhood*. Cambridge, MA: MIT Press.

Carey, S., Evans, R., Honda, M., Jay, E. and Unger, C. (1989) An experiment is when you try it and see if it works: A study of junior high school students' understanding of the construction of scientific knowledge. *International Journal of Science Education*, 11.

Carmichael, P., Driver, R., Holding, B., Phillips, I., Twigger, D. and Watts, M. (1990) *Research on Students' Conceptions in Science: A Bibliography*. University of Leeds: Centre for Studies in Science and Mathematics Education.

Chalmers, A. F. (1982) *What is This Thing Called Science?* Milton Keynes: Open University Press.

Chi, M. T. H. (1992) Barriers to conceptual change in learning science concepts: A theoretical conjecture. *Proceedings of the Fifteenth Annual Cognitive Science Society Conference, Boulder, CO, USA*.

Driver, R. and Oldham, V. (1985) A constructivist approach to curriculum development in science. *Studies in Science Education* 13, 105–22.

Driver, R., Asoko, H., Leach, J., Mortimer, E. F. and Scott, P. (1994a) Constructing scientific knowledge in the classroom. *Educational Researcher* 23 (7), 5–12.

Driver, R., Leach, J., Scott, P. and Wood-Robinson, C. (1994b) Progression in students' understanding of science concepts: Implications for curriculum design. *Studies in Science Education* 24, 75–100.

Durant, J., Evans, G. and Thomas, G. (1989) The public understanding of science. *Nature* 340, 11–14.

Duschl, R. (1990) *Restructuring Science Education: The Importance of Theories and their Development*. New York: Teachers College, Columbia University.

Giere, R. N. (1991) *Understanding Scientific Reasoning*, 3rd ed. Fort Worth: Holt Rinehart & Winston.

Harré, R. (1986) *Varieties of Realism: A Rationale for the Natural Sciences*. Oxford: Basil Blackwell.

Karmiloff-Smith, N. and Inhelder, B. (1974) If you want to get ahead, get a theory. *Cognition* 3, 195–212.

Kuhn, T. S. (1962) *The Structure of Scientific Revolutions*. Chicago: University of Chicago Press.

Kuhn, D., Amsel, E. and O'Loughlin, M. (1988) *The Development of Scientific Thinking Skills*. Orlando, FL: Academic Press.

Larochelle, M. and Désautels, J. (1989) 'Of course, it's just obvious': Adolescents' ideas of scientific knowledge. Paper presented at the first international conference on the history and philosophy of science in science teaching, Florida State University, Tallahassee, November 1989.

Latour, B. and Woolgar, S. (1979) *Laboratory Life: The Social Construction of Scientific Facts*. London: Sage.

Layton, D., Jenkins, E., Macgill, S. and Davey, A. (1993) *Inarticulate Science? Perspectives on the Public Understanding of Science and some Implications for Science Education*. Driffield: Studies in Education.

Leach, J., Driver, R., Millar, R. and Scott, P. (1993a) Children's ideas about the nature of science from age 9 to age 16. *Proceedings of the Third International Seminar on Misconceptions in Science and Mathematics Education, Cornell University, August 1993*.

— (1993b) *Children's Developing Ideas about the Domains of Scientific Investigation from 9–16*. Working Paper, Centre for Studies in Science and Mathematics Education. Leeds.

Leach, J., Driver, R., Scott, P. and Wood-Robinson, C. (in press a) Children's ideas about ecology 2: Ideas about the cycling of matter found in children aged 5–16. *International Journal of Science Education*.

— (in press b) Children's ideas about ecology 3: Ideas about the interdependency of organisms found in children aged 5–16. *International Journal of Science Education*.

McCloskey, M. (1983) Intuitive physics. *Scientific American* 248, 122–30.

Meheut, M., Saltiel, E. and Tiberghien, A. (1985) Pupils' (11–12 years old) conceptions of combustion. *European Journal of Science Education* 7 (1), 83–93.

Miller, J. (1983) Scientific literacy: A conceptual and empirical review. *Daedalus* 112 (2), 29–48.

NCC (National Curriculum Council) (1993) *Teaching Science at Key Stages 3 and 4*. York: National Curriculum Council.

Parusnikova, Z. (1992) Is a postmodern philosophy of science possible? *Studies in History and Philosophy of Science* 23, 21–37.

Pintrich, P. R., Marx, R. W. and Boyle, R. A. (1993) Beyond cold conceptual change: The role of motivational beliefs and classroom contextual factors in the process of conceptual change. *Review of Educational Research* 63 (2), 167–200.

Popper, K. R. (1969) *Conjectures and Refutations*. London: Routledge & Kegan Paul.

Rowell, J. and Dawson, C. (1983) Laboratory counterexamples and the growth of understanding in science. *International Journal of Science Education* 5, 203–15.

Samarapungavan, A. (1991) Children's metajudgments in theory choice tasks: Scientific rationality in childhood. Paper presented to the annual meeting of AERA, Chicago IL, April 1991.

Solomon, J. (1983) Learning about energy: How pupils think in two domains. *European Journal of Science Education* 5 (1), 49–59.

— (1991) Teaching about the nature of science in the British National Curriculum. *Science Education* 75 (1), 95–104.

Solomon, J., Duveen, J. and Scott, L. (1993) 'Students' learning about the nature of science'. *Proceedings of the Third International Seminar on Misconceptions in Science and Mathematics Education, Cornell University, August 1993*.

Songer, N. B. and Linn, M. (1991) How do students' views of science influence knowledge integration? *Journal of Research in Science Teaching* 28 (9), 761–84.

Stavy, R. (1988) Children's conception of gas. *International Journal of Science Education* 10 (5), 552–60.

Thomas, G. and Durant, J. (1987) Why should we promote the public understanding of science? *Scientific Literacy Papers* 1, 1–14.

Vosniadou, S. and Brewer, W. F. (1992) Mental models of the earth: A study of conceptual change in childhood. *Cognitive Psychology* 24, 535–85.